FINANCIAL BLISS

*A Couple's Guide to Merging Money Styles
and Building a Rich Life Together*

Bambi Holzer

AMACOM

AMERICAN MANAGEMENT ASSOCIATION

New York • Atlanta • Brussels • Chicago • Mexico City • San Francisco
Shanghai • Tokyo • Toronto • Washington, D.C.

Special discounts on bulk quantities of AMACOM books are available to corporations, professional associations, and other organizations. For details, contact Special Sales Department, AMACOM, a division of American Management Association, 1601 Broadway, New York, NY 10019.
Tel: 212-903-8316. Fax: 212-903-8083.
E-mail: specialsls@amanet.org
Website: www.amacombooks.org/go/specialsales
To view all AMACOM titles go to: www.amacombooks.org

This publication is designed to provide accurate and authoritative information in regard to the subject matter covered. It is sold with the understanding that the publisher is not engaged in rendering legal, accounting, or other professional service. If legal advice or other expert assistance is required, the services of a competent professional person should be sought.

Library of Congress Cataloging-in-Publication Data

Holzer, Bambi.
      Financial bliss : a couple's guide to merging money styles and building a rich life together / Bambi Holzer.
          p.   cm.
      ISBN-10: 0-8144-0885-0 (hardcover)
      ISBN-13: 978-0-8144-0885-8 (hardcover)
      1. Couples—United States—Finance, Personal.   2. Investments—United States.
3. Financial security—United States.   4. Wealth—United States.   I. Title.
HG179.H59477   2007
332.0240086'55—dc22

                                                                            2006026860

Printing number

10   9   8   7   6   5   4   3   2   1

Family has always meant a lot to me. From my deceased father to my very much alive mother (and, of course, stepdad Jack), I have been blessed. Not to mention Audrey, Len, Margot, and Bette.

Along came my incredible husband Charles, who brought with him a family that I couldn't have been luckier to call my own. Not a day goes by that I don't appreciate my incredible fate in having Ali, Steve, Madison, J.T., and Danny in my life. Then there's the added bonus of Howard and Beverly, Lisa and Marty, and each of their clans. I am truly fortunate.

Charles, keep on doing whatever it is you do to keep me loving you so much, and thanks for making your family mine.

CONTENTS

Introduction   1

As a financial planner and advisor, people come to me to help them devise a strategic vision for their present and future. We grapple with complicated financial issues like asset allocation in the investment portfolios and the like, but in the two decades I've been doing this work, I've come to realize this: Most times the real crux of the matter I have to deal with when I work with couples is a personal issue lurking just below the surface of their financial considerations. One partner is extremely risk averse, while the other wants to strike it rich. One partner might not want to give up their current lifestyle to chase the other's goal of becoming an artist. Another couple might be completely identical financially, leading to blind spots and missed opportunities. Without tackling these issues ahead of time, a perfectly designed and executed financial plan will still not satisfy both partners. My goal is for these couples to become aware of their differences and how they can work through them. They've planned ahead financially and can now benefit from my counsel. I often work with another group of people: Those who've been jolted out of their financial stupor by a life event, frequently one that is out of their control.

One thing that I've discovered over the years is that many of my clients experienced a "green wall of silence" when it came to money matters. In their families, finances were not to be discussed. It was okay to talk about other people and the external expression of their money—what kind of car they drove, where they went on vacation, how they dressed, what their home looked like—but mom and dad never really let the kids in on the family's financial status.

Many of my clients, and many more people besides, take this "speak no evil" approach to financial matters. My own experience was far different—which is why I'm able to connect with my clients and get them to open up. I grew up in a suburb of Chicago in the 1960s and 1970s when moms stayed home and parents felt safe letting their kids wander the neighborhood. My mom was the exception. She went to work for Prudential Insurance when I was fourteen years old. She quickly rose to the top of the sales force, traveling throughout the country giving speeches (she even went outside the United States to speak in Kyoto, Japan) and wrote a motivational book called, *Success Comes in Cans.* Her career choices and career path were truly unheard of at the time, but she was certainly a role model for a lot of women.

What may have been even more unusual at the time was that my parents paid the bills together. I can still picture them sitting down with their checkbooks and their bills in hand—each reviewing all of the expenditures as partners. I don't know this for certain, but I'd guess that most of my friends' parents didn't work as a team. In most households in those days, the woman received an "allowance" from the man—who handled all the financial matters. If the women got involved at all, it was to do the menial jobs like check writing and making deposits at the bank and withdrawing money for household expenses. Back then it was most assuredly the man who made all the serious financial investment decisions. Now, don't get me wrong—I'm not saying I lived a fairy tale life. Just because my parents worked together on financial matters, doesn't mean that they agreed on every point. By and large, mom and dad agreed to disagree about these decisions. They talked about money as being another facet of their relationship. They shared their opinions with mutual respect for one another. And that's the whole point. They discovered what works best for them.

My husband and I also discovered what works best for us. I own my business and my husband is a well-respected radiologist. Being a doctor, he relies on his reputation to attract patients to fill his computed tomography and magnetic resonance imaging machines without any additional marketing or advertising costs. He doesn't understand why I spend so much of the money I earn—pumping it back into the company. As a result, we decided to have separate bank accounts. He pays the mortgage out of his account, and I pay for groceries, entertainment, and travel out of mine. We went with our arrangement because it was more convenient—no major monthly sit-downs to attend. However, just like my parents, we both have to agree on major purchases and, obviously, major investments. We talk freely about our goals and desires.

In this book, you will learn how to work together as a couple to make your financial life more successful. The book's premise is simple.

If you can:

- Understand yourself and your relationship with money.

- Understand your partner and his or her relationship with money.

- Understand the implications and facets of the many financial decisions you will face as a couple.

Then: You will have planned safely for your financial future and the future of your relationship.

Specifically, along the way you will learn how to marry your partner's own tolerance for financial risk with your own and to match your compromises with your individual and shared aspirations at critical life stages. I will also show you how to reach decisions about money in a realistic, nonconfrontational, effective way. Through several quick and easy (but thought-provoking) questionnaires, each of you will figure out your own money personality. We'll probe some of your ideas about money and try to understand why they exist. You'll learn how to improve your financial savvy through some eye-opening and entertaining questions from the field of behavioral finance—the study that examines the ways in which human beings are irrational about money. We'll discuss goals and values. After this self-examination, you'll learn ways to expand your financial comfort zone that you can have productive conversations with each other about your financial life together and come to the decision that best suits both of you and optimizes your lives. Remember, accumulating money is never a goal. Money is merely a tool to use to obtain that which is valuable to you—whether you value material possessions, peace of mind, or passing your wealth on to the next generation.

Throughout the book, we'll follow the fortunes of many of the couples I've worked with. Through their stories, you will see the varied issues that these couples like you have struggled with at every stage in a relationship and examine the solutions that have worked in real life.

Without a roadmap and signs along the way, you would find it very hard to travel anywhere new. In the same way, reaching financial goals requires a map and an organized way of charting your course and progress. We'll look at ways to get your financial lives organized so that you both understand where you are and can track your progress. We'll have you prepared to take control of your financial lives alone if need be so that you don't end up like some of my unprepared clients.

Lastly, I'll update you on the markets and advise you on some changes you can make in your investment strategy. Since my last book, the world has changed dramatically. Risk and uncertainty have escalated in many aspects of our lives with the increased threat of terrorism, natural disasters, and pandemics. Old bromides about the market can't be applied haphazardly under these circumstances. I will show you what will work in today's environment and what can lead to personal financial disaster.

WHAT YOU WILL LEARN FROM THIS BOOK

How to have a better financial relationship with your partner.

- Determine your own "money" personality and style

- Understand the blind spots we all have about money

- Learn how to have productive communications and decisions on money issues

How to organize your financial life as a couple.

- How and when to schedule family financial planning meetings to determine a budget and set goals for saving and purchases

- Essential documents to have on hand

- Worksheets to do and keep updated

- Actions to take

How to work through life stage issues that couples face.

How to successfully invest now.

Remember when you were young and first dating? Remember all the emotional ups and downs you went through? It's like we were all passion addicts when we were younger. We craved that high and wallowed in the low. Remember when you first started earning your own money? Remember how great that feeling of euphoria was as you thought about all the things you could buy with it? We felt so good for those first few moments, days, weeks, and maybe even months when we had our latest possession. Funny thing is, in both of these cases the euphoria and passion didn't last all that long.

Hopefully, as we mature, we realize some things about ourselves and about our relationships with others and with money. Over time, as your emotional and financial maturity has developed, you've come to define bliss a bit differently. When we're younger, it's all about the excitement, the new. Now that we've spent a few more years on the planet, spent a few more years with our loved one, we've come to understand that bliss can mean something else— security. Bliss can mean the security of knowing that we have someone in our life to support us and someone we can support. It can mean the security of knowing we will be able to provide for ourselves and our family through retirement and beyond.

I called this book *Financial Bliss* for a reason. I've come up with a kind of shorthand formula that explains how you can achieve bliss in your merged financial lives:

Knowledge is Power. Power is Control. Control is Security. Security is Bliss.

When I talk about knowledge I mean three kinds of knowledge:

- Of Self

- Of Partner

- Of Financial Concepts

How do you utilize this knowledge and convert it into power? Through communication with your partner, with your experiences, and with experts. Once you have power, you can control your environment. The control that knowledge provides you lessens risk and makes you feel secure. Being free of worry about your finances is the kind of bliss I wish for all of you.

I congratulate you on having the courage to take this next important step in your couplehood. Just like every other step you've taken so far, this one will require some work, but will also provide you with handsome (and a few cute) rewards along the way. I'm so pleased you've decided that bliss is going to be a part of your financial life. I don't know about you, but I'm eager to begin. Let's get going!

GETTING TO KNOW YOU AND YOUR PARTNER

1

LOVE . . . AND DEAD
ENDS . . . ARE BLIND

I normally don't like to do this, but let's face it, the news about the success rate of marriages in the United States just isn't good. So let's deal straight away with the elephant in the room. That elephant's trunk is just one of the pieces of baggage that have an impact on the frankly awful statistics telling us that, even with a decline in recent years, we can still expect roughly one in three marriages to end in divorce. We bring to our legal unions a host of pieces of luggage individually, and it is the rare couple who have a matched set of emotional, sexual, familial, communicative, and financial bags enabling them to build a lasting relationship. You already probably know that sexual and financial differences run neck and neck as the leading wedge dividing couples and causing a divorce. As I said in the introduction, financial matters are highly charged with emotion, nearly as charged as sexual issues depending upon the couple, so it should come as little surprise that many couples are incapable of resolving their financial differences.

This union of marriage and money is not a recent phenomenon, as psychotherapist Brad Salter mentioned to me in a recent conversation. He brought up a little thing called a dowry which to this day, in many cultures, still plays a significant role, symbolic and real, in marriages. That financial exchange or transaction may not exist in the United States in its pure form, but when couples form here today, remnants of that thinking remain. According to Brad Salter relationships are based on dependency needs. He has witnessed a lot of clients, who, as a result of a financial downturn, experience a surge in vulnerability and a lack of control. As their net worth dwindles, so does their self-worth, and feelings of inadequacy come flooding in. As Salter so aptly put it, "Money never made the man or woman, but it has broken them." Another phenomenon Brad has noticed is the number of singles who wait to enter into couplehood until they are financially secure. They want to be as stable and responsible as possible, and often seek mates who exhibit both these traits themselves.

Obvious point number two: Because couplehood* involves two human beings, it takes good communication skills for these unions to thrive and to survive. Since good communication skills are necessary to resolve any conflict, and as the emotional charge rises our ability to communicate effectively falls, is it any wonder that financial conflicts are responsible for a high number of divorces. The news is even worse, since the numbers we have available only account for the number of divorces financial problems cause. What about the number of arguments or unhappy relationships they result in?

Jacqueline Schatz, MA, EdM, LMFT, is a psychotherapist in practice in New York City who specializes in relationship issues. In an interview, she told me that:

---

*For the purpose of this book we will use this more encompassing term since it accounts for state-recognized marriages, same-sex unions, common-law arrangements, and unwed partners who co-habit.

Generally, the emotional issues surrounding money are different for each member of a couple. Thus, money is one of the primary areas around which couples fight and that cause difficulty in their partnership. Couples are actually fighting about their emotional differences but labeling the problem something concrete: money. Without an exploration of the emotional issues regarding money, couples have very little chance of resolving their financial differences or having a successful relationship.

As you'll see later on, when we discuss your Financial First Date, much of what we suggest isn't a debate on the Federal Reserve's most recent decisions regarding interest rates, it deals with how you feel about money. Talking about emotions isn't easy. It requires a certain level of comfort with intimacy.

Here's the good news. Just because you haven't been able to communicate effectively about finances, doesn't mean you *can't*. It simply means that you *haven't*. "Haven't" implies *yet*. Your yet is today. Congratulations on picking up this book as the first (or perhaps next) step in securing the future of your relationship and your finances. By working your way through it, by completing the surveys, worksheets, and goal-setting forms, you will greatly increase your chances of beating the marriage/divorce odds. Here's the warm and fuzzy side of those increased chances of success: You'll have a long and fulfilling life with the love of your life. Here's the down and dirty bottom line: Divorce is expensive.

I'm glad we got that out of the way. As much as I like to dance, the quick step around the truth has never been one of my favorites. It's far too easy to get tripped up and those pratfalls are not only embarrassing, they're downright painful. So let's do what we can to avoid being red faced and swollen kneed, shall we?

Now that we've agreed on that, we can proceed. There's a bit more bad news you're going to have to face. Like most everything else required to make your union last, shaping up financially is going to take some work. The first part of this book is going to be less painful. In it, you're going to take a look at yourself and your beliefs, values, assumptions, and behaviors associated with money. What I'm going to ask you to do isn't physically or emotionally demanding, but it is going to require you to be honest with yourself. There's no point in doing this unless you are going to be fearless in your self-assessment.

I'm going to show you what I mean: I'm really not as smart, rational, and as logical as I think I am. I'll admit my ego stung a bit the first time I learned this, but the fact that I learned it made me smarter, which made me feel better. Knowing that I didn't know everything made me work that much harder to understand what I was missing, revealed to me the blind spots I had to pay more careful attention to, and taught me that when I was really in doubt, I needed to turn to an expert for advice. All of this made me smarter than if I had walked around making all kinds of smart assumptions about myself. See how it works?

How did I learn this painful truth about myself? Before I get to the specifics, let me tell you a little story that proves my point.

An old friend from college recently stopped by for advice. Stacey and I haven't seen each other since our first reunion after college, so we spent some time catching up. She was a political science major in school and was very active in the College Democrats organization and worked on several state and national campaigns. She went on to get her masters in environmental studies. As she updated me on her life, I tried to guess what her job was based on some of her statements. Based on what you know of her, which of these three occupations do you believe is Stacey's?

1. Campaign consultant

2. Environmental lobbyist

3. Retail clerk

What did you guess? Believe it or not, she is a retail clerk. (If you guessed that, I doubt if your reasoning matches the explanation as to why that was the most logical guess.) Given just the information provided above, I jumped to conclusions. She has a master's degree, she was politically and environmentally active, and so on. It's a no-brainer right? Well, if, like me, you chose 1 (or even 2) you also ignored the biggest part of the problem-solving equation. Did you factor in that there are 8,200 times more retail employees than registered environmental lobbyists in the United States? (According to the Center for Responsive Politics, from Senate Office of Public Records data, there were 1,878 registered environmental lobbyists in 2005; whereas Department of Commerce data indicates that there were 15.4 *million* retail employees in 2004.) Considering this fact, the chances were 8,200 to 1 that she would be an lobbyist rather than a retail clerk. In fact, there are 500 times more Wal-Mart employees than registered environmental lobbyists in this country. I had fallen victim to one of the many blind spots that we all develop in trying to make sense of our complicated world. I ignored the odds—the base rate. I took a shortcut in order to make a quicker decision, and that shortcut missed important information. You all know the old saw about making assumptions and what that makes you and me. Welcome to the club. It's not a very exclusive one, but at least you won't ever lack for company.

So what does Stacey's employment choice have to do with you and your finances? Well, the kind of thinking (or lack thereof) that you did in choosing which of the three careers Stacey had can creep into your financial decision making. You may be making assumptions when you think you are making informed decisions. The problem is that your information may not be correct. Keep in mind also that you had no emotional investment in this decision, so, theoretically at least, you were operating at the peak of your capacities for objective reasoning. And you only had to choose from three options. What happens when the choices are more varied and the stakes are higher? How do we behave when we are making financial decisions?

That's the focus of the burgeoning field of study called behavioral finance. On scales small (individual) and large (stock market investors, for example), behavioral economists track and try to make sense of the decisions we make with our minds and our money. For example, economists and stock market theoreticians have long wondered why the efficient market theory doesn't seem to hold all the time in real life. In other words, why doesn't the market always go up on good news and down on bad news? Why are some days of the week better than others for buying stocks? Why do people not always make decisions that are in their best economic interest? From these initial questions first seriously studied in the late 1960s, the field of behavioral finance has conducted a wide range of studies to understand why we as individuals and as an economy don't do things by the book.

What these researchers found seems pretty obvious once brought to light, but has complicated economic forecasting by adding elements of psychology and probability that had not previously factored into its calculus of the economic order of the world. Calculus and order are very different from the messy world of people and their minds. For individuals, it means that we now have names for some of the economic decision-making maladies we carry around in our brains. Now that we have identified them, we can try to compensate for them. That's the point of this section of the book. When you identify the tendencies and characteristics of your own economic decision making, you can avoid the pitfalls, turn your weaknesses into strengths, and, most importantly, understand for yourself and explain to your partner why you made a particular financial decision.

How many times have you witnessed your partner make a purchase decision that seemed the epitome of stupidity or that utterly disregarded your feelings? Well, by understanding and applying some of the principles of behavioral economics, you will understand that what appears to be the result of stupidity is simply the result of a faulty basis in reasoning. Would you rather have someone say of a choice you made that it was (a) stupid or (b) based on faulty reasoning? It's not just a question of semantics or making nice. When someone's reasoning is faulty, it can be corrected objectively. That's especially true because if you are the faulty reasoner, you won't be as defensive as you will be if you're identified as being "stupid."

So, before your partner gets a hold of the book, let's take a look at a few scenarios so you can see how your financial reasoning ability stacks up. I'm not encouraging competition here, mind you. Just trying to give you a leg up.

HOW OBSERVANT ARE YOU?

When I was a kid, I loved the children's magazine *Highlights*. One of my favorite activities was doing the "What's Wrong with This Picture?" page. Here's a slight variation on that activity to measure how observant you are:

> How many times does the letter *f* appear in the following sentence?
>
> The functional fuses have been developed after years of scientific investigation of electric phenomena, combined with the fruit of long experience on the part of the two investigators who have come forward with them for our meetings today.

The letter *f* appears _____ times. (Answer below.*)

*   *   *

One thing behavioral finance has taught is that we all tend to overestimate our abilities generally, and one mark of our thinking

*11 times. (Most people miss the *f* in "of.")

abilities is our power of observation. A good defense lawyer knows this, and despite what we've come to think of the importance of an eyewitness in prosecuting a crime, witnesses are among the least reliable bits of evidence available. As humans we are very prone to errors in our observation or to simply not being observant enough.

MAKING ASSUMPTIONS

Which is the more likely cause of death in the United States—being killed by falling airplane parts or being killed by a shark?

* * *

__ Falling airplane parts
__ Shark

* * *

Because the media sensationalizes fatal shark attacks, or simply because it reports such attacks at all, most people select shark attack as the more likely cause of death. The truth is that for approximately every one person killed by a shark, thirty people will die as a result of falling airplane parts. When given a choice we tend to select the familiar. In this case, if we had taken into account how many are exposed to sharks each year (those who live near or travel to the coast) and how many are exposed to falling airplane parts (not geographically dependent to the same degree) we would have realized that a greater percentage of the population is at-risk to airplanes than sharks. Logically then, in the absence of any other data, the correct choice would have to be airplane parts.

MAKING ASSUMPTIONS
ABOUT OURSELVES

So what if you didn't count all of the *f*'s or didn't know that airplane parts can be killers? After all, in the world of knowledge these are slightly more important than parlor tricks or bits of trivia to fascinate (or bore) coworkers. Where behavioral finance crosses the line from minutia to matter is when it helps us to understand how we perceive ourselves generally. Later on in this chapter you're going to be asked to engage in some self-assessment. It's important that you know up front that you are biased. Like the vast majority of people, you will rate yourself more highly than an objective third party would. On the one hand that's good—self-esteem is important. On the other it's important to recognize that you have this bias.

For example, in a study of one million high school students, it was learned that 70 percent rated their leadership as above average; only 2 percent rated themselves as below average in this trait. More interestingly, 100 percent of those surveyed rated themselves as easier to get along with than their peers. Similarly, a survey of university professors revealed that 94 percent of them felt they did a better job of teaching than their colleagues. Clearly, we can't all be leaders, can't all do a better job than everyone else, and we can't all be that easy to deal with. The numbers just don't add up. The point is clear: we overestimate our abilities. How many people do you know who admit being a bad driver? It's always the other guy's fault, right?

Where this overestimation of abilities gets really interesting is when we are asked to self-rate. The table below reflects just how pervasive this optimism concerning performance is. A group of freshly minted college business graduates at two different universities were asked to self-assess and rate their business acumen versus their fellow graduates—not based upon their grade point average, which would be fairly easy to assess, but their overall business skills, something they could use their ego to evaluate. In the first column is a list of the percentiles into which the graduates could place themselves—from being in the top one percent of the graduating class to the fiftieth percentile. In both cases, they clearly overrated their own performance. You can't have 8 percent of the total graduate population performing in the top 1 percent. The numbers just don't work that way. Interestingly, in both cases, none of the graduates rated themselves below the 50 percent mark. Someone has to be rated that low, but who really wants to admit their performance is that poor?

Percentile Categories	School A 268 total grads	School B 445 total grads
Top 1%	8.0%	11.9%
Top 5%	32.4%	42.0%
Top 10%	61.8%	73.3%
Top 25%	89.7%	92.5%
Top 50%	99.6%	100%

Clearly, it's someone else who isn't carrying their fair share of the load. I don't know where the idea comes from that it's very lonely at the top. This makes it look pretty crowded up there.

ARE YOU SURE?

What's also interesting to note is that behavioral economists have discovered that as our self-expressed certainty goes up, the likelihood of our being right goes down. In other words, the more certain we are about something, the greater the chance that we will be wrong. How many times have you heard yourself say after finding your keys in your purse or a pocket, "I was absolutely certain I set them down right *there!*" and pointed to another location? When people are 99 percent sure of themselves, they are right about 70 percent of the time. I could live with being right that often, but again what's important to note here is the discrepancy between what we believe about our selves, our abilities, and our answers and reality. How does this tie into finances? Well, consider the number of shares of stock that are traded on the New York Stock Exchange each day. Each of those shares represents a choice, a decision someone made. As you've probably figured out by now: we don't always make good choices in dating partners or dividend providers. Here are some interesting insights into trading:

A study of 6,000 brokerage accounts and 60,000 trades (from 1991 to 1996) discovered that after factoring in trading costs:

- The average return for investors was well below standard benchmarks.

- Investors who traded most, earned the lowest average returns.

- Stocks they bought performed worse in the next year than the ones they sold did.

- Men trade more and earn lower returns on average than women.

Clearly, we aren't able to invest on our own as well as we think we can, and our decisions are clouded by human emotion.

SOME DOLLARS ARE MORE VALUABLE THAN OTHERS . . .

It's your tenth anniversary and you've scored tickets to a play your partner has been talking about for weeks. They cost you $300, but you know your partner will be thrilled. On the night of the performance you approach the entrance to the theater only to find that you don't have the tickets. Do you go to the ticket booth and buy two more tickets?

* * *

☐ __ Yes
☐ __ No

* * *

Now let's change the scenario a bit. You didn't purchase the tickets ahead of time. You had arranged to buy the tickets from someone once you got to the theater. That night, when you park your car you find that you lost the $300 you had in your wallet. Do you find an automated teller machine and buy your tickets?

* * *

☐ __ Yes
☐ __ No

* * *

I'll bet your answer is different for each of the scenarios. If you are like most people who answered a similar question, you'll probably *replace* the tickets if they are lost but won't *buy* them if you lose the money to pay for them.

Why?

Rationally, you have lost $300 either way—whether in the form of paper money or in the form of theater tickets—and it will cost you another $300 to replace them. But we put our money into separate little vaults in our minds and some vaults are emotionally worth more to us than others. For most people, it feels worse to lose the tickets if they've already been in your possession than it does to lose the money you were going to use to pay for them. Yet, when adding things up to figure out your net worth at that point in time, the $300 reduction in your net worth is the same either way. For some reason, it hurts more to lose the actual tickets than it does the money. While there's no right or wrong answer to the question above, you should have the same answer to each question if you're thinking logically.

Did you get that one right or are you not convinced? Try this one. You worked hard this month and as a bonus your boss adds $2,000 to your month-end paycheck. You've been eyeing a $2,000 big-screen television for a while, but aren't convinced you can afford it. Do you buy it now?

* * *

☐ — Yes
☐ — No

* * *

Now instead assume that you won $2,000 on the lottery last night. Do you buy the television?

* * *

☐ — Yes
☐ — No

* * *

Lastly, assume you just got a letter from your credit card company raising your limit by $2,000 and offering an outrageously low interest rate on upcoming purchases. Do you buy the television?

*   *   *

☐ __ Yes
☐ __ No

*   *   *

Most people would view lottery winnings as mad money to splurge with. Credit card debt comes in second as unreal money and so it too is more easily spent. But money earned from hard work just seems too valuable to part with that easily. Bills and savings for college or a new home seem to be the only things worthy of such hard-earned cash. Yet, whether coming into your possession through hard work or good luck, money is money. Attaching any sort of extra value to some of it isn't sound economic thinking. Yet, we all do it. None of us want to break into our childhood piggybank full of money from cutting lawns to pay for that new bike, but without a second thought we'll gladly use the birthday money that comes every year from Aunt Martha.

Let's go back to the theater ticket example—only this time you haven't lost them. You also have made reservations at a wonderful French bistro that has been earning rave reviews and has few openings for dinner through the end of the year. For some reason, your partner takes offense at your attempts at humor at very poignant spots in the play and decides the evening is over at the first intermission. Assuming the evening won't go any better either way, do the two of you go on to the restaurant so as not to lose the limited opportunity or do you head home?

*   *   *

☐ __ Stay
☐ __ Go

* * *

You've already wasted a good bit of money on the theater tickets ($300) for a show you only saw half of. What are the chances that you'll be able to salvage the evening by spending forty-five dollars on *foie gras* appetizer and another hundred on a good bottle of Merlot? No one is betting on you even getting to the main course at this point. But a majority of people responded that they would go on to the restaurant. Why are we so prone to throw the proverbial good money after bad? Rationally, the ticket money is gone no matter what. The remaining dinner money could stay in our pocket to be spent on something of greater value than a cold shoulder. Yet we'll spend it to try to save some value from the ticket expenditure. It can't be done. The ticket money is gone forever. We should try to save what remains of our money (and our relationship) and move on. Economists call this the sunk-cost fallacy. To reason properly, you should consider that money already spent is gone and should not be factored into future decisions.

Here's one that's a little more complex and has much greater repercussions.

After a great year at work, your boss surprises you with a $10,000 year-end bonus. The only stipulation is that you must invest it in one of the annuities an affiliated company offers. Annuity A is guaranteed to earn 5 percent ($500) the first year. Annuity B has a 50 percent chance of earning 10 percent ($1,000) and a 50 percent chance of breaking even. Which do you choose?

* * *

☐ __ A
☐ __ B

* * *

How about if Annuity A is guaranteed to cost you $1,000 with no return and Annuity B costs you $2,000 but has a 50 percent chance of earning zero (net, you lose $2,000) and a 50 percent chance of earning $2,000 (net, you break even). Which do you choose? Research by behavioral economists using similar questions find that most people would choose Annuity A in the first example and Annuity B in the second. We all hate to lose money, and in the first example Annuity A's guarantee is enticing. The 50 percent chance of not making as much money as we could otherwise sounds too risky. If you look closely at the probabilities, however, A and B are equivalent. In the second example, A and B are again equivalent. Annuity B, however, has that chance of making more money. We're willing to gamble on the upside if our downside is covered. This loss-aversion syndrome carries over into many decisions we make, financial and otherwise. Part of it may be our lack of knowledge regarding probability and in some cases probability is difficult to define, but even in carefully constructed tests with precise probabilities, most of us prefer to forego an upside gain in order to protect ourselves from loss.

The outcome of the previous example isn't dependent on one's knowledge of probabilities, but it might be instructive to review how these probabilities are calculated.

In the previous example, Annuity A has a fixed outcome, so probabilities are irrelevant. For Annuity B, two different outcomes are possible. Multiply each outcome by its probability (its chance of occurrence) and add the outcomes together to find the expected value of the annuity—what it is worth given the possible outcomes.

	Possibility 1	Possibility 2	Expected Value of Annuity B
Outcome	−2,000	0	
Chance of Occurrence	50%	50%	100%
Expected Value	−1,000	0	−1,000

The total chance of occurrence will always be equal to 100 percent—there's a 100 percent chance that *something* is going to happen. If you have ten possible outcomes, the total of the possibilities for each will still equal 100 percent. And each outcome doesn't have to have the same possibility of occurrence. Think of poker and the various possible hands, from two of a kind to royal flush, and the chances of drawing each. And you see that the expected value doesn't correspond to either of the actual outcomes. It's the average of all the outcomes.

	Possibility 1	Possibility 2	Possibility 3	Possibility 4	Expected Value
Outcome	−5,000	0	2,500	50,000	
Chance of Occurrence	10%	20%	50%	20%	100%
Expected Value	−500	0	1,250	10,000	10,750

What's the point of all this? If you have alternatives to assess, the only way to standardize their value and make a rational decision is through use of the expected value.

Lack of knowledge of probabilities also comes into play in choosing mutual funds and other choices. Hot hands, momentum, and streaks have been debunked by statisticians. Even flipping a coin and counting heads or tails illustrates that streaks of some length can occur even though the chance of each throw turning up heads or tails is 50 percent. Streaks of six, seven, and ten in a row are statistically more common than you would intuitively expect. We expect to see a random alternating pattern, but in the short-run, probabilities allow for streaks. In basketball, an 80 percent free throw shooter could hit twenty in a row and his or her performance would not be an anomaly. But over the long run, heads will show up 50 percent of the time and the free throw shooter will revert to his 80 percent shooting average. Similarly, in any given year about half the managers beat the market and half trail the market. (In reality, all managers don't manage the same amount of money, so it isn't exactly half.) A three- or five-year study of a manager's returns isn't indicative of a manager's prowess. Some studies have shown that ten or more years may be how much data are needed to make a judgment.

You've just inherited a substantial amount of money from your great uncle. He bequeathed to you 5,000 shares of General Electric stock he held for some time. The trustee has contacted to ask you what you want to do with the money. Taxes and transaction costs are irrelevant. Which option would you choose?

1. Retain the 5,000 shares of General Electric, a stock of moderate risk with a 50 percent chance that over the next year its price will increase by 10 percent, a 20 percent chance that it will stay the same, and a 30 percent chance that it will decline by 2 percent.

2. Sell General Electric and invest the proceeds in the shares of ABC Incorporated, a more risky stock with a 30 percent chance that over the next year its price will triple, a 40 percent chance that it will stay the same, and a 30 percent chance that it will decline by 40 percent.

3. Invest in U.S. treasury bills, with an almost risk-free return of 4.4 percent over the next year.

Most people would choose to keep the General Electric shares. Why mess with a good thing? Actually, option 2 has the highest expected return, option 1 has the second highest expected return, option 3 has the lowest expected return but with no risk, but most people would rather maintain the status quo than switch—this is known as the devil you know versus the devil you don't syndrome. The "status quo effect" keeps you in a bank certificate of deposit even though you know you could make more elsewhere. It keeps you from switching health insurance providers or even financial advisors because switching takes some effort and increases uncertainty. But even in controlled experiments with a better outcome as a certainty, respondents choose the more comfortable status quo over an option that would be better for them. Inertia requires people to exert a powerful force to overcome it. The longer we sit idle, or in the same position, the harder it becomes to move again.

Similar to the status quo effect, the endowment effect keeps us anchored to our present circumstances. Being a season ticket holder, you have tickets to the first game of the World Series. Your job requires you to be out of the country that day, so you cannot go. You decide to sell the ticket. How much would you ask? Instead, now imagine that you don't have a ticket, but you really want to go. How much would you be willing to pay someone for a ticket? I'm sure that, like nearly everyone else, you would want to sell your ticket for more than you would be willing to pay to buy one. Psychologically, what we have is worth more to us than what we want. We all know people who ask too much when they try to sell their home or car but turn around and disparage the price their neighbor is asking for their nearly identical home or car. For some reason, we think that our ownership of something imbues it with added worth. That might be the case if we are a celebrity, but for the rest of us we merely drive economists crazy with our irrational expectations.

YOU PAID *HOW MUCH* FOR THAT?

This concept offers some insight into the kind of thinking that goes into our purchases and price tolerance. Has your partner ever come home with something and you've asked the question above? Well, this may help explain why he or she did what she did.

How much did your first home cost you? Got a ballpark number? Okay, what was the median cost of a four-bedroom home in this country in 2000? What's your answer? By asking the first question, I've set an anchor for your answer to the second question. No matter the first question, it nearly always affects the respondent's answer to the second question. Anchoring is used in sales, parlor

games, and negotiations to move an answer away from the respondent's intuitive answer and toward the questioner's objective. Without the amount of your home purchase being entered into your
consciousness, your answer most likely would have been vastly different than it was. For that very reason, car makers assign a sticker
price to their vehicles, though the assumption we all have is that's
not a fixed price. It does however serve as an anchor—it's the point
around which the negotiations will revolve.

In financial situations, we anchor our willingness to pay on a list
price or what someone else paid and not on the object's actual
value. Market bubbles occur because groups anchor on what others
state is the value of something and then determine value from that
point. If an analyst said that a stock was worth $50 last year, and it
beat estimates it must be worth $50 plus $X now. Rules of thumb
also act as anchors. You come up with a best guess answer using a
rule of thumb, and then the rest of your analysis is done with an
eye toward staying close to that rule of thumb number that should
have no validity when you dig deep. Budgets almost by definition
have anchors—last year's budget. And they just keep escalating.
Only with zero-based budgeting—starting from scratch to rational-
ize almost every dollar spent—can true efficiency be realized. We'll
talk more about this when we discuss budgeting and goal setting.
By the way, the median cost of a four-bedroom home in 2000 was a
little over $209,000.

We use anchors in our daily lives as well. For example, my husband loves to go to Las Vegas and gamble. I don't see the thrill of
it, but he's an adult and he never goes overboard because he's got
a self-imposed anchor around his neck—and he's not a very strong
swimmer. So, he goes to the craps tables and tells himself that he
has a cap above which he will not go. If he loses that amount he
quits. The difference between a gambler like my husband and a
gambling addict is that my husband's anchor stays firmly in place.
Now, I use anchors when I'm shopping. I walk out the door of my
house knowing that I want to buy a new coat, but I'm only willing

to spend X number of dollars on it. If I'm being good, I don't go above that amount. Later on we'll talk more about couples and spending patterns and strategies, but as a preview to that discussion you should know that my husband and I each agree that we have our own "mad money." We don't have to be accountable to one another for how we spend it or why we choose to spend it that way. I don't get the gambling, but I don't have to. What happens in Vegas stays in Vegas, but what I buy at Nordstrom's comes home with me.

PRIMACY, RECENCY, AND FREQUENCY

Have you ever noticed that once you buy a certain car you see more and more of them on the street? Or how about a new sweater? Our consciousness becomes alert to things that have been already brought to our attention. In decision making, we tend to be swayed by the viewpoint that gets the most hits. Supporting the old contention that even bad publicity is good publicity, we do create a bias for those things that are on the top of mind. We might not know the exact details, but we know we've heard of it. In weighing decisions, opinions or ideas that have many "hits" usually trump those that have fewer. Apparently, the more support we remember for an idea the more reasonable it becomes. So, when it comes time to buy a compact disc player, are you going to buy the most reliable one, the one that best fits your budget, or the one that you've been bombarded with by television ads?

And what do we tend to remember? We remember things we saw or heard first (that's primacy) or last (recency). Repetition (frequency) also enters into this, but in general keep this in mind: What's at the top of our mind isn't always the most useful material for decision making. How many times have you asked yourself: Why did I think of that?

Let's end this chapter with a little fun. The quiz in Figure 1-1 tests your general knowledge. You don't have to guess the right answer. You only need to pick a high and low number to create a range in which you feel 90 percent comfortable that the actual answer falls. For instance, to the question "What year did WWII end?" your answer could be 1940 on the low end and 1948 on the high end. You are 90 percent confident that the actual date is within this eight-year period. Now try these questions. Remember, you are looking for a range within which the answer will fall.

FIGURE 1-1. Financial knowledge quiz.

	90% Confidence Range	
	Low	High
1. Amount the average American loses gambling each year		
2. Percentage of total purchases made in America by women		
3. Number of people in America who own two homes		
4. The number of millionaires in America		
5. Number of billionaires in the world		
6. Number of billionaires living in New York City		
7. Percentage by which the stock market performs better on sunny days than on cloudy days		
8. One share of Berkshire Hathaway stock sold for $18 in 1965. What was the cost of one share on December 20, 2004?		
9. What is the estimated average credit card debt the American family carries?		
10. What is the highest income tax rate (%) imposed on Americans today?		

Ten questions. You only had to guess with a 90 percent confidence interval, so you should get nine of the ten right. Do you think you did that well? Here are the answers:

1. $350.00

2. 85 percent

3. 6.4 million

4. 2.27 million

5. 691

6. 34

7. 25 percent

8. $86,300

9. $8,000

10. 10.37 percent

Don't fret if you didn't get nine out of ten. Multiple studies have asked groups of experts, from MBA candidates to brokers, questions about their own fields and they missed half or more even when given wide confidence intervals. We all overestimate our knowledge; as a result, our overconfidence can lead us to make mistakes. Because we think we know it all (or a large percentage of it all), we don't do enough research or we employ anchors and rules of thumb as shortcuts.

In addition, we often think that our individual experiences are representative of the wide possibilities actually obtainable. We trust our intuition or the intuition of experts without actually tracking how well that intuition has done in the past. I don't want to scare you into indecision, but I do hope that you remain alert. More important for our purposes, I hope you realize that you don't have a corner on the market of financial acumen. Stay open to the ideas and methods of your partner as you go through this process together. Before you judge your partner's ability to make sound financial decisions, make sure you understand your own thought processes and misses.

In the next chapter, we'll continue this self-exam by focusing not just on how you think, but on how you behave.

FINANCE IS IN THE EYE OF THE BEHOLDER

Our Individual Money Styles

etty and Joe are a fairly typical couple when it comes to money discussions. They either don't talk about their finances at all or only do so when circumstances force them to. Invariably, they end up arguing or with hurt feelings. Buying a car, deciding how much home they can afford, how lavishly they can spend on a vacation, and how much and where to invest are all discussions that happen only when the occasion arises. Too often, their discussions degenerate into emotional outbursts and one of them either storms off or quietly acquiesces. Decisions never come easy. As we mentioned earlier, studies have shown that money issues, either directly or indirectly, are a leading cause of divorce. And greater riches don't immunize you from problems. In fact, they may make problems worse.

As we've seen, for many of us, money is as emotionally charged a subject as sex—and just as mysterious and taboo as we grow up. Many times, we can't discuss it because we really can't put into words why we feel the way we do and where those feelings come from. Hopefully, chapter one gave you a foundation for understanding how and why you make some of the decisions you do. In this chapter, we will build upon that foundation to show how you present those financial predispositions to the world through your money personality.

As children, we get random signals from the way our parents respond to our requests for things and some of the conversations we overhear about the family situation, but rarely are any of these overt, consistent, or well thought out. We never seem to understand the true reason we can't have that toy we so desperately need or why mom is going back to work. We haphazardly learn about the social and emotional value of money, and we rarely learn how to handle it wisely. As therapist Jacqueline Schatz points out, "Parents often believe they are protecting their children by not discussing financial issues with them. Yet, when these children become adults themselves, they may be left with an immature understanding of money and no real tools for handling finances or for knowing how to communicate about finances with a partner." So how do we have this kind of financial communication with our children? What do we do in a world that is materially obsessed? This is a frequent problem for many of my clients who live in affluent communities. No matter what values they espouse at home, what they see on television, and how their classmates and friends conduct themselves, sends a contradictory message.

I do have one client who was born and raised in the Midwest and subsequently moved out to Los Angeles, where he lived in an affluent neighborhood devoid of ethnic or economic diversity. He didn't want his children raised in that kind of isolated environment, so he searched high and low for a home in a more ethnically and economically diverse neighborhood where they could attend public school. He wanted to keep his kids grounded—rearing them with Iowa values and experiences.

A MONEY TEMPERAMENT QUESTIONNAIRE FOR COUPLES

Let's face it, you wouldn't be reading this if you and your partner were in perfect agreement on all things financial. That you don't have perfect congruency is to be expected. Jacqueline Schatz shared a story with me that nicely illustrates how different two couples can be:

> I once worked with a newly married couple who both came from families in which the fathers were in charge of all financial matters. This couple assumed this was the way to do things and naturally repeated the pattern in their marriage. They came in to see me because the wife discovered that the husband had gotten far behind on the bills. She was confused as to why her husband was not handling the bills better, as her father had, and she was scared for their future. In exploring their personalities, stark differences were revealed. The husband was an artist. He was extremely creative, thought "outside the box," and was not interested in the day-to-day details of money and time frames. In contrast to her husband, the wife (a nurse), was realistic and detail oriented. She was able to juggle multiple tasks with accuracy; however, she was not as imaginative as her husband. I helped the couple to take on their financial decision making and bill-paying tasks as a joint venture, utilizing both their different temperaments and skill sets. Eventually, they learned to create a new family model, different from their families of origin, their own version of a successful union.

It's my hope that if you and your partner both take this assessment seriously, that you'll be able to recognize the important temperamental differences and use them to their best advantage.

We need to be honest with ourselves and our partners about our relationship with money—what tools and information we use to make money decisions. Without such self-knowledge and sharing, we will always have money fights and self-inflicted money problems. At the very least, we won't deal with issues well and reduce the chances of reaching our goals.

The first step in the process is to determine your money style. We won't deal with the whys yet, but merely look at your attitudes and behaviors. The purpose here is not to explain or change, merely to recognize. Your money style consists of how and why you spend money, how you make decisions about it, and what it means to you. You need to recognize your style and identify what your partner's style is in order to make better decisions together. Once you realize how each of you operates, you can work better as a team. Later on, we'll show you how you can engage in productive discussions about how to accomplish your financial goals. Remember, though, there are no right or wrong answers. So, no defensiveness, criticizing, ridiculing, or attempts at re-educating. Your objective is to listen and understand so that a good partnership can be created. You are not trying to convince or to change each other. You want to work toward an understanding of each other and gain a level of comfort openly discussing these issues, so that when money matters arise you will get ideas on the table and mutually and strategically develop a plan rather than deal with issues by default.

FINANCIAL TEMPERAMENT QUIZ

To complete this quiz (see Figure 2-1), simply rate how well each statement applies to you. Be truthful and answer how you really

FIGURE 2-1. **Financial temperament quiz.**

	Statement	Answer	Trait
1	I must have the best of everything even if I can't afford it right now.	_____	A
2	I usually end up selling my investments too soon. They continue to rise after I sell.	_____	D
3	I can walk away from a deal that isn't just right even if I really want it.	_____	E
4	You can't make money without taking risk.	_____	C
5	I like a steady paycheck even if I don't make as much as I could.	_____	D
6	I buy things for myself to cheer myself up.	_____	F
7	I let my partner handle money matters.	_____	G
8	To be successful, you must look and play the part by living in an exclusive area and having expensive things.	_____	A
9	I believe that I can usually beat the odds when it comes to financial matters.	_____	C
10	I like to analyze the pros and cons of important decisions.	_____	E
11	I don't have the time or energy to worry about investing. I'm too busy trying to make money.	_____	G
12	I'm pretty good at sticking to a budget.	_____	E
13	I'd travel out of my way to get a good deal.	_____	B
14	You have to save money to make money.	_____	B
15	When I've hurt someone I like to buy something special for them to show I'm sorry.	_____	F
16	I might do some analysis, but I prefer to then let fate help me decide what to do.	_____	G
17	I like to shop where the service is best.	_____	A
18	I avoid doing my taxes until the last minute.	_____	G
19	Risk doesn't really exist if you know what you're doing.	_____	C
20	I feel guilty spending money on myself.	_____	F
21	I could probably afford a better car.	_____	B
22	Being too conservative with your money is worse than taking some risk.	_____	C
23	I prefer safe and conservative investments. I'll do okay in the long run.	_____	D
24	I'll buy something even if it's more than I wanted to spend just because my children and spouse want it.	_____	F
25	I could make the time, but I pay to have my car washed, house cleaned, and lawn mowed.	_____	A
26	I can't bring myself to buy the most expensive item once I decide I need it. I'll buy the lower-priced version.	_____	B
27	I like to go shopping just because I have nothing better to do.	_____	F

28	I feel overwhelmed by financial matters and rely on the advice of others if I do anything at all.	____	G
29	Utility is a given. I want beauty in my belongings.	____	A
30	I want to be in a job where my income is unlimited even if it's volatile.	____	C
31	If it's not on sale, I don't buy it.	____	B
32	I need to check my investments often to make sure I'm not falling behind.	____	D
33	I control my money. It doesn't control me.	____	E
34	Sooner or later, something will go wrong so it's best to prepare now.	____	D
35	I like to make financial decisions on my own; otherwise, I feel pressure to do what others want.	____	E

Totals for Each Letter Category

Total for A _____   **Total for B** _____   **Total for C** _____   **Total for D** _____
Questions 1, 8, 17, 25, 29   Questions 13, 14, 21, 26, 31   Questions 4, 9, 19, 22, 30   Questions 2, 5, 23, 32, 34

Total for E _____   **Total for F** _____   **Total for G** _____
Questions 3, 10, 12, 33, 35   Questions 6, 15, 20, 24, 27   Questions 7, 11, 16, 18, 28

feel, not how you think you should feel or how you think you'll score the best. There is no best score. The scale goes from 1 to 4. Use 1 if the statement is "not me at all" and 4 if it "absolutely describes me." There is no neutral midpoint, so you have to commit one way or another. Put your answer on the line to the right of the question. Later on, you will total up the scores you have placed in the boxes labeled with an A, B, C, D, E, F, or G.

In this quiz, we are measuring three important aspects of your money personality. We are looking at how you view the utility or purpose of money, your comfort with risk, and finally, your decision-making style.

For example, if you look at the answer column, you will see that a letter is in each answer space. Those letters correspond to one of the traits we are measuring. You should total your score for all of the "A" questions (1, 8, 17, 25, 29). Since there are five questions corresponding to A and the maximum score you can record on the line next to each question is 4, the highest possible score you can have is a 20. Since you cannot score a 0 on any of the lines, the lowest score you can put is a 1. Therefore the lowest possible total score for any letter is 5. Your score must be between 5 and 20.

The quiz has measured your financial style on three important dimensions of your relationship with money. In the table in Figure 2-2, the scores in the first two columns help to define your view on the utility of money. The second important dimension, reflected by your scores in the next two columns, is your comfort with risk. Lastly, you need to understand the factors you consider when making financial decisions—your scores posted in the last three columns give us some indication of your tendencies in this area.

MONEY IS THE ROOT OF ALL . . .

To better illustrate my points, the names and characterizations of the types that I've given represent the far ends of the spectrum. Rarely will you find a person who fits such extremes. Most people will fall somewhere in the middle—in fact, at one time or another, we all exhibit traits of each of the types. Also, please keep in mind that no type is better than another. Each has pros and cons and may be more or less effective than the others in some situations. Each merely represents one way of relating to money.

FIGURE 2-2. **Your financial temperament profile.**

	A	B	C	D	E	F	G
4.0							
3.0							
2.0							
1.0							
	Ritz-Carltons	Econo Lodgers	Texas Slims	Worst-Case Scenarists	Data Darlings	Drama Kings and Queens	Ostriches

| **Utility of Money** | **Risk** | **Decision Making** |

The first two columns in your scoring chart reflect your attitude about the utility of money—in other words how it should be used and what purpose it should serve in your life. In this regard, I've found that people fall into two categories. Ritz-Carltons view money as a way to enjoy life now. They tend to spend today and let tomorrow take care of itself. They require comfort and luxury above all else and feel that they are entitled to both. Somewhat stereotypically, you might imagine a trust fund baby as a kind of extreme example of a Ritz-Carlton—someone like Paris or Nicky Hilton. So are your other young, idle, unemployed gossip page types. Lavish surroundings and a more public display of their wealth—or the high level of wealth they wish to eventually attain—are priorities. Ritz-Carltons believe that associating with people of equal or greater financial stature is a vital tool to lift themselves into the upper echelon. For Ritz-Carltons, a budget is a foreign concept—like an exotic vacation they've heard of but believe has no appeal.

Keep in mind that these terms are all relative. You don't have to have the money that Donald Trump has in order to be a Ritz-Carlton. You just have to spend a larger percentage of your income on so-called bling than you do on practical items. In other words, you can earn like an Econo Lodger but still spend like a Ritz-Carlton. That's where credit card debt comes into play. It's not always what it seems. You don't necessarily have to be wealthy to dream about how you would spend it. We are endlessly fascinated with the wealthy.

Econo Lodgers are at the other end of the utility spectrum. They are frugal and self-sufficient. They won't pick up the check, but they won't stick you with it either. Having items be of use and serving their purpose well is more important than having the finer things in life. Why buy a brand-name product when a generic one will do? Better yet, why buy it at all if they've gotten along without it so far? They believe that rainy days eventually will come, so they had better save now so that they can weather the storm later. They have simple needs and wants and avoid any hint of ostentation. They might be able to spend money on others, but they definitely find it difficult to spend on themselves. They are good at sticking to their budgets and take as much pleasure in the deal they've found than the item they've purchased. Jack Benny worked hard to earn a reputation as the most miserly of men, and he projected a lifestyle of an Econo Lodger even though he was quite wealthy.

Once you've figured out your spending personality, you need to consider your risk tolerance. These scores are plotted in columns three and four of Figure 2-2. Some correlation exists between spending styles and risk tolerance, but it isn't as strong as you would think. I've had clients who fell into the Ritz-Carlton category but were very risk averse. They wanted to live well now so they overextended themselves on their consumer borrowing, but their investment portfolio was very conservative. They somehow thought of the two money styles as completely unrelated.

Within the category of risk, a number of distinct personality types lurk. Texas Slims thrive on risk. These gambling types feel that they must take big risks to make big gains, and the risk is always worth it. They are sometimes blind to risks. They only see opportunity. The downside of any risky choice only happens to other people. They will play a hunch or overextend themselves financially without a well-thought-out plan. I had one client who insisted on risking it all on a natural gas deal that never fired. He lost it all. He very quickly went from being the most Texas of Slims I knew to our next category—after losing big, he was afraid to repeat that nightmare. And a nightmare was lurking around every corner.

On the other hand, Worst-Case Scenarists see risk in everything. They would prefer a world with no risk, where everything is guaranteed. If it can't be guaranteed, then it's too risky for them. "FDIC" and "Full faith and credit of the Government of the United States of America" are not sufficient comfort for them. They must know all the issues and monitor things closely in order to feel even a small amount of comfort. They may even want to do everything themselves. A very successful entertainer has come to me to help him handle his finances. It turns out my job is very easy. Because his family lost a great deal of money in the stock market, he insists that I do nothing but put his money in bank certificates of deposit and in treasury bills. To this gentleman, safety and security are more important than return on investment.

The final dimension is which set of filters you use to make a decision.

When it comes to making money decisions, what I call Data Darlings employ pure rationality. If they can't reduce a choice to numbers it shouldn't be part of the decision matrix. If the numbers don't work, they don't do it. Needs and wants are nice, but if they don't fit into the five-, ten- or twenty-year plan they've formulated, they ignore those desires. They keep debt to a minimum, not because of the risk but because it diverts them from their goals. They seek and destroy any hint of emotion. If they do things by the book and use self-discipline, they will reach their financial goals. They've yet to meet a research challenge they weren't able to live up to. Sometimes they can go a little too far. I have one client who is a highly educated professional. He thinks he can use that marvelous brain of his in every situation. Unfortunately for him, he suffers from paralysis by analysis. By the time he does all his research, frequently the opportunity to invest has passed him by. It's great to consider all the angles, but sometimes the Data Darlings' number crunching can bite them in the assets.

Drama Queens/Kings, by contrast, let emotion trump rationality. Their feelings and the feelings of those around them dictate their decisions. Whether to please others or to seek revenge, they feed off their current emotional state when deciding what to do with their money. Shopping becomes a tonic to be applied to hurt feelings. A new high-definition television or pair of shoes validates their self-worth. I recently had a client call me from Neiman Marcus in Beverly Hills. She told me that she'd had an argument with her son over a new girlfriend of whom she disapproved. She was already $7,000 into her retail therapy by the time she called.

Unlike the other dimensions, in decision making we have a third style that could potentially be a part of our financial personalities. Some people fall into the Ostrich category. They aren't somewhere between Drama Queens and Data Darlings. They don't even register on that scale because they've decided to completely avoid getting in the game. They feel so overwhelmed by the financial aspects of life that they just confer control to others. Sometimes it's a partner or a trusted professional, but at other times Ostriches give power to an inexperienced friend or even a boss. They just want to be done with it and let someone else worry about it because they can't. They might be trusting, they might feel that they don't have the knowledge, or they just don't want to be bothered because the rest of their lives take up so much time or emotional effort. Whatever the reason, they relinquish control to others.

I recently had a very bright young man come into my office. He had just inherited a fairly sizable amount of money from his grandfather. I sat him down and started to talk to him about his options, what his goals were. After a minute, he dropped his head and stared at his shoes. He held one hand up like a traffic cop. "You don't understand. I don't want to know. You do it." And that's what I did.

Some Ostriches may not give total control to others, but they still refuse to deal with some money issues. For instance, they may continue to put money in a passbook savings account because their parents did or they always have, even when their wealth has passed the point of such an account being appropriate for them. They can't or don't want to deal with making any changes, so they decide by defaulting and make no changes at all.

As I said earlier, none of these styles is completely right or wrong. Each may be more or less suitable given the circumstances. The idea is to understand your style and be aware that valid alternatives exist. Add a little flexibility to your viewpoint and accommodate your partner's approach. For instance, an Econo Lodger/Ritz-Carlton couple can still work well together. The Econo Lodger may be in charge of the budget, but the budget may incorporate a little more discretionary expense than the Econo Lodger would normally prefer. The Ritz-Carlton partner can be in charge of that aspect, and as long as the Ritz-Carlton partner stays within parameters, the Econo Lodger can accept a little luxury in his or her life.

Each of the styles might try to incorporate a little of the other's tendencies into their position. Data Darlings might try to add a little bit more risk to their portfolios. Take 10 percent of your individual retirement account and put it into something with higher potential gains. Do your research and understand the risks, but try to focus a little more on the possibilities. Econo Lodgers could add a little flavor to their lives. Enjoy an occasional night out or update your wardrobe a little bit at a time. Don't look at it as money thrown away but as an investment in yourself—a livelier attitude or more updated approach might open up new opportunities.

There will always be exceptions. I have a very dear client who is a dyed-in-the-wool Econo Lodger with Worst-Case Scenario tendencies of the highest order. Yet, when it came time for her daughter's wedding, she was emptying the vault and spending like the best Ritz-Carlton out there.

GENDER AND MONEY

It should come as no surprise that men and women behave differently and hold different views when it comes to financial matters. Just as the personality types discussed above provide a general outline of characteristics, the conclusions we can draw about gender differences are generalizations more than precise measurements of differences. Some studies have shown that men tend to be more risk tolerant than women. In many ways, this makes sense. Men are socialized to be more adventurous in most areas of their lives. In addition, for many generations of men and women, it was the man who was the traditional breadwinner and the one who handled the finances and made most of the decisions. I'd be risk averse too if someone else were making most of the decisions for me, if someone else were responsible for making sure that my children and I were fed and clothed, and if I felt that my fate was in the hands of someone other than me. Even today, in most American households, women are prone to defer to their husbands in financial matters. Gender and finance is a fascinating subject, but keep this in mind: No matter what I say about who makes the money decisions, men and women are equally capable of making good and poor decisions about their financial futures.

SO, WHAT'S IT ALL ABOUT?

Knowing your own financial personality type, how risk averse you are, how you view the utility of money, and the decision-making style you generally employ, is just the first step toward achieving financial bliss. You've established a base line of data for yourself. If you learn that you're a financially risk-averse person, it is worth spending some time considering what has influenced you to be this way. Again, this isn't about cleaning out your closet to rid yourself of any financial ghosts that may lurk there, it is about understanding the nature of your behavior, assessing whether your behavior, beliefs, and attitude are working for or against you. At the same time, it's also important to consider your partner. Does your partner share traits with you? How have your partner's experiences shaped him or her? What is the nature of those experiences?

While we can discuss some of these issues in the context of this book, much of this is homework that you need to do together independently. We're not talking about fruitless navel-gazing here (unless you choose to stare at a navel orange), we're talking about an honest self-evaluation, individually and collectively, to better understand how you got where you are financially, where you want to get to, and what changes you need to make (if any) in order to reach your goals.

Before we get to that next phase in this process—the goal setting, it is essential that you stake out your present territory. Settle in and look around and then discuss with your partner the various factors—inherited family values, money myths, and so on that have shaped your beliefs and influenced your actions. For example, I have a client, Karen, who is extremely conservative when it comes to matters financial. She told me a story about her father who, after church services on Sunday, drove around their midsized suburb and pointed out various opportunities he passed on—a bank he could have invested in, a housing development a friend could have gotten him in on the ground floor of, a fast-food franchise that was now booming. Although her father never said why he passed on all of these chances, the answer was implicit—because they all involved some kind of risk that he wasn't willing to take. Another element of her father's story was even more insidious. Other people were meant to succeed. Other people were somehow lucky. They were willing to take a chance, but I couldn't do that and risk the future of my kids and my wife. You don't put your own needs and desires ahead of anyone else's.

It was only after Karen and I had several conversations that she understood the powerful influence her father's after-church sermons had on her—and how her brother Sam heard the same stories but walked away with a distinctly different message—life should not be about could haves, should haves, or any other form of regret.

Some people choose to impart more positive and affirming lessons on their children. I have a friend with several children. One year for Halloween, shortly after they'd moved into a new neighborhood, they miscalculated the number of kids who would stop by their house. Within a half-hour, their supply was nearly out. She thought about sending her husband out to get more, but just as she was about to tell him to go, her own kids came back from their round of trick or treating with bags bulging. She sat them all down and told them about the importance of sharing and how giving a gift to others is one of the best gifts we can give ourselves. The kids agreed to contribute their candy to the cause, and every year after that, they've upheld this tradition. Similarly, another client takes her kids with her on her monthly volunteer efforts at a downtown soup kitchen. Those kids have come to appreciate what they have and how much more fortunate they are than most.

To better understand the powerful effects of the money lessons you learned so far, let's look at some basic questions. For now, you are to consider these questions privately. Later on, we are going to ask you and your partner to get together and share responses to some of these questions. For now, consider this the pre-interview phase. We are going to ask you and your partner to schedule two meetings. The first will be your Financial First Date, and the second will be your Financial State of the Union Meeting. As you can tell just from the names of the meetings, the first one is going to be a more fun, information-sharing kind of meeting, and the second will deal with more specific issues. We don't want you to walk into either of these meetings unprepared; thus, the lists of questions that follow.

WHAT DO YOU LIKE ABOUT MONEY?

So far, we've figured some of your money "what's"—what your attitudes, behaviors and values are. The next phase is to dig a little deeper into those what's but to also come up with some why's and how's. For example: What does money mean to you? Love, safety, happiness, power, freedom, self-worth? Why do you feel that way? How were your beliefs and values about money formed?

We live in an extremely materialistic country. As a child or young adult did you grow up wanting or were most of your material needs met? Did your parents lavish things on you in place of time or attention? Did you feel deprived or guilty based on what you lacked or what abundance you enjoyed? What is important for you to accomplish in your life? What is important for you to have? What is important for you to be?

I know some people for whom being wealthy is their main goal in life. I know others who say that it's important that they be passionate about their work and the money issue is secondary. The point of this book is not to judge you but to help you understand yourself so that you can realize your goals. Without thinking about your money-related values and beliefs, you will be in reactive mode instead of being able to stick to a plan. Without knowledge of your feelings, your partner will not be able to support your efforts. And without a discussion between the two of you, it's unlikely that either one of you will be able to meet your goals. You will be in reactive mode and turmoil will occur every time money comes up.

Separately, each of you should look over the following list of questions that probe your values, goals, and views on money. Not every question will spark a deep discussion, some are meant to stimulate ideas rather than be directly answered. But don't skip one because it doesn't come quickly to mind as important. Digging a little under the surface might bring up thoughts or feelings that end up being very important both to you and your relationship. After some reflection, schedule time to talk about your thoughts.

What are some of the "money messages" you live by? Where did they come from? Have you reexamined them lately to see if they still are, or ever were, valid?

- Growing up, money was _____? What was the money situation at home? What are some of the ideas about money you heard or surmised? In your family, what did money symbolize? Love, power, security, self-worth, evil? How do you think this may color your ideas about money now?

- In your previous significant relationships, how was money handled? What did you fight about? What did you learn from those experiences?

- Did you ever feel guilty or ashamed about how much or little money you had?

- Do you have any specific money memories that left a lasting impression on you?

- If we truly love each other, we won't fight about money.

- If we don't talk about money, everything will work out okay.

- The hardest lesson I've had to learn about money is . . .

What is important to you? Have you thought about your goals and values, and have you incorporated them into your financial life?

- I am . . .

- I enjoy . . .

- I believe . . .

- I am afraid of . . .

- I seek . . .

- I want money because . . .

- To feel that my life has meant something, I need to . . .

Rank the following items in order of importance to you:

_____ Exotic Vacations

_____ Children's College

_____ Nicer Home

_____ Cars

_____ Investment

_____ Retirement Planning/Saving

- If I won $200,000, I would . . .

- If I won $200,000, I would feel my financial situation was . . .

- What is important enough to me that I would risk our current financial situation on it?

- What is so important to me that I would work sixteen-hour days (or put up with my partner working that much) for the extra income?

- I feel it is my job to be the breadwinner. If I couldn't I would . . .

- If my partner could no longer contribute to the income, I would feel . . .

- If my partner made more money than me, I would feel . . .

- If our income was cut by one-third, what would I give up first? What would be untouchable?

- If our income rose by 50 percent, what would be the first thing I would do?

While the questions above are speculative and deal with possible future outcomes, the reality is that you are already engaged financially with another person. Consequently, it's important to pay attention to these more practical questions about your present financial situation. Here, we are making a move away from the self-assessment portion of the program to specific issues that you should discuss at what we're going to call your initial Financial State of the

Union Meeting. We'll go into more detail about this meeting in the next chapter. Consider these the pre-interview questions you are asking yourselves before that face-to-face meeting takes place.

- Who keeps track of the checkbook, pays bills? Why?

- Our current net worth is . . .

- Our fixed monthly overhead is . . .

- We spend our discretionary income on . . .

- I know whether or not we have together or separately a will or living trust . . .

- I know how much we need to save each month for tuition, retirement, and other goals . . .

- I know enough about our insurance, investments, and other financial matters that if my spouse should die I can take over full management of my financial life . . .

Obviously, we've given you many, many questions to think about. It is probably neither practical nor possible to cover all these issues at one time. However, it is important to deal with when you do hold your first financial summit meeting. Think of that meeting as the first formal exchange of information between two great countries, two great companies, or two great institutions who are considering merging completely, establishing trade agreements, or otherwise engaging in commerce with one another. We want you to first be as prepared as possible and to have thought as deeply as you can about yourself and your money habits, beliefs, and values.

The next step is to explore the ways in which your partner's habits, beliefs, and values, jibe with your own. We'll turn to establishing the common ground needed for such an exchange in Chapter 3.

"WE NEED TO TALK"

O kay, so far we've put you through your paces to show that money is a difficult issue for people to talk about and share with one another. We've gotten you to realize that people often overestimate how smart or rational they are. We've also helped you to identify what financial temperament you have in terms of three dimensions—you're view on the utility of money, how willing you are to take risks with your hard-earned (or even inherited) cash, and what approach you take to making financial decisions as an individual. So, are you feeling blissful right about now? Not so much, right?

Well, hang in there. Things are about to get better. How can I say that about a chapter with this title? I know that no four words can strike as much fear in the heart of a romantic partner as "We need to talk." That statement can set up a cascade of recollections of dissolutions and early heartbreak, memories of being called on the carpet by your parents or teachers, or someone delivering us bad news about a loved one's health. Words carry an emotional weight, and just as its important to think about your own money style, it is equally important to think about your own communication style.

Bob and his wife Charlotte are what most people would consider a fun couple. Bob is a former college football player turned successful medical supply salesman selling computed tomography and magnetic resonance imaging machines to hospitals around the country. Charlotte works in marketing for a major financial institution. Both of them spend their days talking to people—sometimes at other people, sometimes with them. Bob is about as garrulous and glib a guy as you'd ever like to meet. The first time I met him, I was reminded of the actor John Goodman from the show *Roseanne*. He had that "guy from next door" charm and an easygoing demeanor that belied his six foot four, three hundred–pound presence. Still, lurking somewhere beneath that veneer of laid-back good guy gentility was the heart of a competitor, a closer. Whenever we sat and chatted he was affable and smiling, but when we started to discuss any of the fine points of his financial plan, his eyes grew more intense, his pronunciation more precise, and a filter limited the number of words he used—he didn't want to be placed at a disadvantage by saying too much.

Charlotte on the other hand, was a classic "yacker." No detail was too small, no bit of trivia too minor to avoid passing from her brain to her lips. Fortunately, she had such a pleasant lilting speaking voice and a soothing demeanor that you seldom noticed that she was going on and on. When the two of them were in my office together, I noted a hint of Bob's exasperation with his wife's tendency to "overshare." His eyes would narrow and his glance would drop to the floor, and I could almost imagine each of the digits between one and ten forming themselves in the veins in his forehead. I noticed immediately that Bob had the habit of following up many of Charlotte's comments with, "What my wife is trying to say is . . ." A red flag to be sure, and one that got waved frequently.

Another client of mine, a lovely couple in their early sixties, consists of another dominant male at work who makes most of the financial decisions while his wife sits on the sidelines. That's why I was so surprised one day when the wife set up an appointment to talk with me about her 401(k). She was a few months away from retirement and wanted to speak to me about rollover options. Her husband didn't attend, but I didn't think that much of it, until the next day, after she and I had made all of the plans. Later, she called to tell me—quite sheepishly—that her husband had been upset that she'd come alone. She told me that he demanded that I cancel all of the transactions until I spoke with him. Clearly, these two needed to do some talking.

THE FINANCIAL FIRST DATE

So, when I suggested that the two of them schedule a Financial First Date, they looked at me a little bit funny, but with a sparkle in their eyes. I told them that, even though they'd been married for twenty years, they were going to step into a time machine and imagine that they were going out on that first date. Only this time, the focus of the first date was going to be on their financial lives prior to meeting one another. They were to assume that they were each a blank slate to the other—they didn't know anything about their past experiences with money. The point here was to share information and stories so that they could get a fresh portrait of what each of them brought to the union. I had to lay down a few ground rules and agenda points for them, because we all know how first dates can go.

- Don't be too concerned about making a good impression and trying to be the person you think the other person wants you to be.

- Impress the other with your honesty and willingness to share and dig deep.

- Look for common ground while still appreciating your differences.

- Avoid the joyful "You like tomatoes? I like tomatoes, too!" response to superficial points of common interest that first daters fall into. While you're fondness for members of the nightshade family* is wonderful and all, keep in mind that nightshade family members are poisonous and a false sense of commonality can poison a relationship as well.

- Be polite, respectful, and charming while still keeping in mind the first point above.

Go for the good night kiss and ask for the next date. Don't make vague, "I'll give you a call some time" promises. Actually schedule your next date. This can either be another sharing session, or, if you feel you've covered all you need to cover at this stage, you can make the big leap into couplehood and schedule your initial Financial State of the Union Meeting.

THE FINANCIAL
STATE OF THE UNION MEETING

Frankly, I was a little worried about the outcome of Bob and Charlotte's first date. I was concerned if it would accurately reflect what they both felt and believed. I had to trust that they could communicate openly and honestly, and I gave them a few guidelines for how to conduct it. I led them through a few of the questions you've already seen at the end of Chapter 2, explaining how these were to be a nonjudgmental starting point.

---

*Yes, tomatoes are a member of this infamous family—feel free to use this bit of trivia as a date conversation starter.

Remember, the point of this first date is to share experiences and to gear up for your next major in-depth discussion of your finances. We all love to tell stories about ourselves and that's what you should be doing here. Unlike a real first date in which those experiences can range from grade-school memories of the time you bought your first pair of jelly shoes to a college cross country driving trip, the focus should remain on financial issues. Don't become the topic police and insist that every word be pertinent to the discussion, but don't let it wander too far afield either.

For couples who have one or both partners who've been members of another couple previously, you can break one social date rule: Please do discuss your past partners, how you felt about how the two of you handled your finances, and so on. This shouldn't turn into a dumping session in which you get to vent about all the bad things about your ex; again, try to keep it focused on money and how you felt about your role and how those experiences shape your beliefs, values, and actions now.

WE NEED TO TALK—BETTER

Another primary goal of this financial first date is to help you communicate about money. After this nice and easy first discussion, you should work on improving your communication skills about finances at every opportunity. Talk about the decisions you made—even if it's to skip that six-dollar double-café double latte in favor of a less expensive iced coffee as your midmorning pick me up. Not to beat a proverbial dead horse, but as we all know, people often struggle with communication. As you saw with Charlotte and Bob, he was never content to let her words speak for themselves, he was always trying to convert them into his. Bad habit, bad communication results. I know that communication theorists suggest that you repeat in your own words what someone else has said to make certain you have communicated effectively—shared meaning—but Bob's intent was to clearly put his imprint on everything Charlotte said. So, before we get too far into the preparations and anticipation of that first date, let's review, or perhaps even introduce some important points to keep in mind about communicating effectively. I don't want to put a damper on your enthusiasm at this point, but remember, understanding each other's attitudes isn't the same as acceptance or acquiescence. Inevitably, issues will arise and strong feelings on both sides will trump understanding and lead to the need for negotiation. In this chapter, I'll expand on the ground rules given in the last chapter to provide you with ways to have productive discussions about important issues that may be bothering one or both of you and holding you back from resolving issues and moving ahead in your financial quest.

The methods outlined in this chapter have proven helpful to many of my clients and I offer them as one way to overcome the communications pitfalls involved in creating and managing your financial life together. Some of you may already have a method that you have found useful in other aspects of your relationship. Whether from experience, sessions with professionals, or from the vast literature dealing with communications, if you already know it works for both of you I encourage you to adapt it to your financial life. From John Gray's *Men Are from Mars, Women Are from Venus* to Deborah Tannen's *That's Not What I Meant* and *You Just Don't Understand: Women and Men in Conversation*, much has been written about effective communication and the factors that get in its way. As a lay person who has needed to help clients in one specific area, I feel able to offer the following suggestions, but relationships with wider issues than what we are dealing with here should certainly seek the input of mental health care professionals. As the psychotherapist Jacqueline Schatz pointed out to me in an interview, "The primary problem couples state for entering couple's therapy is *poor communication*. Without good communication, other aspects of the relationship can break down, particularly over such emotionally laden issues as money. Effective communication is a learned skill and most of us need some work in this area."

WHERE SHOULD WE GO ON OUR FINANCIAL FIRST DATE?

While much thought and planning often goes into a first social date, for your first financial date, don't get too elaborate. Trying to discuss your financial past and your attitudes while on the Eiffel Tower munching escargot-to-go, isn't a good idea—you'll be too distracted. I suggest staying at home, far away from distractions like the kids, the phone, and the television. This should be a nice, casual, and comfortable get-together. Don't make it on a Friday night, unless that's the only option you have, because you'll both be tired after a long week of work and may be tempted to give short shrift to the task. Keep in mind that it's a bad thing to keep postponing a first social date, and you don't want to bail too often on your commitment to going on your first financial date either. Constantly waffling about the location, time, duration, and so on indicates that you're not ready for this kind of financial commitment yet and are likely to have an unproductive meeting.

For now, we'll avoid the question of what to wear.

WHAT SHOULD WE TALK ABOUT?

This shouldn't be a problem. That's why we gave you all those pre-interview questions. For the Financial First Date, I recommend that you don't bring along this book as a reference. The last thing we want you to do is to go through each of the questions in order. First, it would take you hours to get through all those questions; second, in order to get through all those questions quickly, you would skimp on the details and only superficially address the issues. Discuss those questions which, during the pre-interview reading phase really elicited a strong response in you. Also consider raising those questions to which you had a very neutral or nearly absent response. Why? Because a blank or a blind spot in your experience could offer some revealing insights you can use later on.

You want the conversation to flow naturally and spring from issues and ideas that matter strongly to you. You won't be tested on any of this material and levity breaks can be good when inserted judiciously. That doesn't mean only women named Judy may make jokes, but close. Seriously, humor works. I can't stop myself!

HOW LONG SHOULD THE FIRST DATE LAST?

That depends on you. We're looking here for depth of insight not volume of insights. In other words, don't think that exhausting yourself or your partner and then drowning them in a sea of verbiage or driving them insane with a water torture of warbling will win the day. I'm a realist. Most of you have children and lives to lead and you won't devote hours and hours to this enterprise of sharing. Setting a time limit, say, an hour, may make sense for you. Some of you may find that instead of making the big elopement move to holding your first Financial State of the Union Meeting, you may want to have a couple of more "first" dates. That's fine. Remember, most people would rather talk about anything else than money. As a result, this ice-breaking step is essential. It can set the tone for the rest of your financial life together, or it can reduce the chairman of the Federal Reserve to tears.

CRYING! THERE'S NO CRYING ON THE FIRST DATE

Tears of joy are okay. Other tears, not so good. The point to remember here is that as much as we want this first date to be pleasant and enjoyable, once you start to share your feelings and perceptions and beliefs honestly, you are bound to encounter some potential for conflict. As much as we'd like you to limit your discussion to events that took place before the two of you met, we realize that there are limitations to this approach. If you find your conversation wandering a bit over the line (couples who already have a long history together are most susceptible to this), and you begin to talk about the tendencies you've noticed in one another in your time together, or stories about each other's present spending, you need to keep a few other points in mind.

Just because one of you has voiced an opinion or has strong feelings about something does not mean that the other must or will give in or tiptoe around an issue. Workable compromises are still necessary in order to make your partnership more solid and your financial life more effective. Feelings buried or denied will eventually come to the surface with even greater force than they initially warranted. At that point, more effort may be required to diffuse the issue and more damage is possible.

Should you bring up everything that bothers you, no matter how small? Know when to pick your battles, but trust your instinct. If your reaction is strong or you feel that it is important to the relationship, it is probably worth dealing with in a positive way. If it's something that you feel is your issue and less important, and you think you can deal with it on your own, maybe it's worth mentioning but not escalating into a large discussion. By mentioning it to your partner you might find that your partner is willing to compromise or change.

Dealing with nonconfrontational issues can benefit from use of these methods. For instance, when sitting down to discuss life insurance or investments, adhering to these ground rules can help you stay on task and be more positive and productive. Rather than deteriorating into an avalanche of accusations and hurt feelings, you can stay positive and accomplish your objective. You won't have to deal with hurt feelings and other problems afterward. It may not be a point of contention—just something that needs to be dealt with.

The ground rules set out for the Financial First Date certainly apply to any couple's communications. Let's reiterate those rules:

- Above all else, winning the argument is not the objective. There are no right answers, just workable compromises.

- Show that you care for each other.

- Show that you're listening and that what your partner is saying is important to you.

- Do not blame. "I" statements, rather than "because you" indictments, go a long way in reducing resentment and hurt feelings.

WHAT'S NEXT?

Once you've ended the first date, take some time to digest what you've learned. This time off is not to let lingering resentments fester, but to give both of you a chance to think about the various issues you've raised. For some it's a cooling off period, for others, a moment of placid reflection, and for the really fortunate, a moment to bask in the sunshine of your compatibility. As I mentioned before, don't rush into anything prematurely. If you feel like you still have more issues to discuss or you feel you need clarification on some of the positions or beliefs your partner has, certainly schedule another sharing date. The rules are the same, the focus may be more intense on certain issues, but the goal is the same: to better understand your partner's financial predispositions and your own financial predispositions.

Two caveats: First, some may be tempted to use the additional dates as a means to delay the heavier lifting you're going to have to do when you hold your Financial State of the Union Meeting. Second, don't use the additional meetings as a way to exert your will over your partner. The object here is not to convert your partner into a mini-you. Instead, it is simply to understand one another and treat this meeting as a way to establish a base line of data about each other. It should also make you feel more comfortable talking about finances and prepare you for the harder work yet to come.

For those who feel that they've gotten that solid base line information and established a level and tone of communication you both feel comfortable with, the next step is to schedule that Financial State of the Union Meeting. We give it that grandiose sounding name mostly to distinguish it from the more touchy-feely intention of the Financial First Date. It should be a bit more serious because you are going to be doing some serious thinking and evaluating about your mutual financial future.

WHEN TO TALK AGAIN

If either of you feels that the Financial First Date did not go well, you need to set up a follow-up date. For example, one of you may feel that you dominated the conversation that first time "out." Perhaps that's because it is one partner's nature to be more open and chatty; perhaps the other person was simply very reluctant to divulge any information or was having a hard time taking this whole process seriously. No matter the case, if either of you left the first date—or in the days following it came to feel—uncomfortable or uncertain about any of the issues raised, then by all means hold off on proceeding to the Financial State of the Union Meeting.

What you may lose in time at this stage you will gain in productivity down the line when you've eliminated those obstacles to clear communication and shared perceptions of your financial goals and abilities. If you learned something about your partner's past that seems to have a significant impact on them and you didn't know about this coming into the first meeting (for example, his or her parents once had substantial holdings in the stock market but lost nearly everything because of a downturn in the market), you'll need time to digest that information. If you don't deal with the issues arising from this revelation, it will lurk in the shadows of any future conversations and spring out at inopportune moments—often derailing more serious discussion and plans. Better to come to a resolution about this issue before proceeding.

Unlike the First Financial Date, you'll have many conversations come up randomly throughout the course of your couplehood. A missing receipt, a large purchase without your partner's prior knowledge, gift-giving, vacation planning, investment choices, car buying, tax time depression, and any number of other issues create crevasses from which the beast can rear its ugly head. That's why we have you schedule your talks ahead of time—this will lessen the anxiety level. When these unexpected conversations become necessary, the second that the issue comes up may not be the right time to confront your partner. Usually, you're at the height of your emotional response to the issue and may not be at a place in which you can rationally explain your point of view or accept your partner's viewpoint. You may not have the full story and you may not have let it percolate through your reason and psyche long enough to have a well-thought-out position. On the other hand, waiting too long might reduce your recall of the specifics or lead you to feel as if you're ignoring the situation because it wasn't really that big of a deal. And if you wait for the action to occur again, you risk creating heightened feelings of being wronged and less tolerance for compromise.

As a general rule, acknowledge that there is an issue and what emotion you are feeling about it (hurt, anger, and so on), but request a later time to talk about it when both of you have time to assess the situation more clearly. At the least, wait until after the heat of battle to have a discussion. Ask your partner if now is a good time to talk about the issue. If they say it isn't, accept that and request another time that will work for both of you. Don't have the discussion at the kitchen table while one of you is buried in bills or prospectuses. Don't use the clichéd "fine restaurant breakup discussion" method, but you do want a receptive, positive, and undistracted mind on both sides of the discussion. Walking the dog, gardening, doing the dishes, or other activities that take your mind off everyday stresses can facilitate open discussion. Hopefully, you know yourself and your partner well enough to find or create such an environment.

HOW TO HAVE THE TALK—PART II

Once you get to the second conversation, it's not time to unload on each other. Throwing a ton of facts and accusations at someone will not usually foster cooperation. You're not trying to coerce a confession from your partner, so "Good Cop, bad cop" and all the other schemes used on television crime shows aren't appropriate here. Care and protection of the relationship and reaching a workable solution agreeable to both of you is the overriding objective.

Have the proper mindset throughout:

- Believe and act as if a win-win is possible.

- Assume that negotiation is the only necessary channel and that it will work.

- Agree to try.

- Accept equal responsibility for changing your lives or coming to an agreement.

- Be realistic.

Start the discussion by having each of you offer some positive comments about the relationship, not phony comments but real ones that somehow relate to the issue at hand. Next, it is probably best to allow the sender, the person who raised the issue, to start by stating the situation and her feelings. The receiver, the other partner, should listen without interruption except for mirroring or asking for clarification. The objective is to get the issue on the table as clearly as possible so that both of you can respond effectively. Once the sender announces that she has finished, the receiver responds with her feelings and facts regarding the issue. Again, the idea is not to tear down the other's argument or convince the other that she is wrong, it is merely to get the necessary information out. Each partner's feelings are certainly part of the information required to create a workable solution.

After the opening statements, discussion of the issues occurs.

- State how you feel and own those feelings. Blaming those feelings on someone or something else is not productive.

- Never use the confidences of previous conversations against each other. You will destroy any trust you have earned.

- Be honest with each other. It doesn't pay to withhold or fabricate feelings or facts.

- Raise the issue in a nonconfrontational way. Use "I" statements. Avoid overemotionalizing and overpersonalizing.

- Do not be defensive or accusatory.

- Don't threaten, bribe, or extort.

- Do not interrupt.

- If you're on the receiving end, verify statements and your understanding of them.

- Thank your partner for confiding in you and valuing the relationship enough to raise the issue.

- If tempers flare, take a break.

- Don't negotiate before feelings and facts are aired out.

LET THE NEGOTIATING BEGIN

After facts and feelings have been expressed, it's time to negotiate. A huge body of work exists on how to negotiate effectively. Some take the approach of how to manipulate to win and get your way, others look for ways to create a win-win situation. Please seek a win-win. You are not negotiating with terrorists or a car salesman or even an irrational toddler. Even then, winning through manipulation is likely a pyrrhic victory—whatever you might gain is lost in destroying your partner's trust, in damaging their feelings. Next time out, you're likely to face a seriously resentful adversary with a chip on his or her shoulder likely to crush you. It's just not worth it in the long run.

> Remember: You are dealing with your life partner and strengthening that partnership is the ultimate goal.

The misleadingly named *How to Argue and Win Every Time* by Gerry Spence has a section on how to negotiate with a loved one and find a win-win. Roger Fischer, a preeminent scholar in the field, and his Harvard Negotiating Project have several great books available. *Difficult Conversations: How to Discuss What Matters Most*, gives a proven step-by-step approach for how to have those tough conversations with less stress and more success.

Among the many great insights the authors offer is something they call "the third story." This "story" is not a reflection of your point of view or of your partner's point of view; instead, the third story represents the difference between those two points of view. By looking closely at how your attitudes, values, beliefs, or even factual assessments differ, you can gain a better understanding of yourself and your partner.

Besides consulting the sources I mention above, here are some additional tips on conducting conversations:

- Don't assume they meant to cause the outcome you perceive. Separate the intent from the impact, and try to explore the intent.

- Make sure feelings are expressed by all parties or they will sabotage the outcome.

- Forget about blame. Blame is judging. Look for contribution—the factors that contributed to the issue.

- Remember, you can't change other people. They are more likely to change if they think we understand them and if they feel heard and respected. They are more likely to change if they feel free *not* to change.

- Don't make statements disguised as questions.

- Don't use questions to cross-examine.

- Start your story with what matters most, the heart of the matter for you.

- Be clear in your statements, don't leave things open to (mis)interpretation. Don't try to soften the message or deliver through hints and indirect statements. Make it clear.

- Don't present your conclusions as "The Truth."

- Don't exaggerate with "always" and "never."

- Give them room to change.

- Don't give in just to move on. Feeling victimized will not solve the issue. Work through it.

In the end, write down the mutually acceptable agreement you've arrived at so that you both ensure that you have understood each other. You should talk until both of you accept the way it is written. This is not a method to hold someone to a perceived contract but a way to ensure that you both understand what was said. Words have different connotations to each of you, so approving the wording forces you to discuss those differences and understand each other's points more clearly. Later on, you don't want to have, "I thought you meant . . ." discussions.

When you finish, share positive comments with each other and celebrate a successful move forward in your partnership.

Clearly, if you find yourself holding your seventh First Financial Date, and keep encountering hurdles to overcome, it may be time to seek outside help. The kinds of communication difficulties you encounter in dealing with your finances may occur in other parts of your relationship as well and need addressing.

Once you've gotten over the remaining hurdles, its time to prepare for that Financial State of the Union Meeting.

CONDUCTING YOUR FINANCIAL STATE OF THE UNION MEETING

J ust like the real thing held in Washington, D.C. every January, your Financial State of the Union Meeting is both a chance to reflect back on your accomplishments and to reveal your plans for the future. While you may not get to walk down the aisle exchanging partisan glad-handing with your fellow party members, have your goals statements interrupted by standing ovations, or have plants in the balcony to bolster your approval rating, you still should approach this meeting as though it matters. In truth, it really does matter. The two of you made a commitment to one another and entered into a social and in some cases legal commitment. Now you've decided to take the next step to secure your financial future together. Whether you are soon to be married, newlyweds, about to celebrate ten, twenty, or fifty years of wedded bliss, a gay couple enjoying the benefits of newly legal recognition of your union and rights, or a cohabiting couple, you can benefit greatly from taking this next step in your lives together.

Take a moment to reflect on what you've accomplished, look back on the journey you've taken together, and think about what you want your future together to look like. You've had a good run so far, and it's clear that if you've gotten this far in this book, you're committed to having an even brighter future—a blissful one at that.

READY, SET, WAIT JUST A SECOND HERE . . .

Before you hold your Financial State of the Union Meeting, you need to have a mini-meeting to determine who is going to be responsible for completing these two tasks:

1. Determining your net worth

2. Tracking expenses for one month

Hopefully, you will agree to work on these tasks together. While the actual completing of the forms we ask you to fill out isn't a very arduous task, gathering the data is time consuming—unless of course, you are extremely organized. At the very least, you need to have access to:

- Statements of bank and credit union accounts: checking, savings, and term accounts

- Statements of investment accounts, including any mutual funds or annuities held outside your brokerage account(s)

- Statements of retirement accounts, including 401(k) plans, IRAs, SEP-IRAs, and any pension or profit-sharing plans

- Recent tax returns

- Statements from your mortgage holder reflecting current balance

- Utility bills

- Credit card statements

- Statements from your auto loan(s) provider

- Life insurance policies

I hope this won't be a treasure hunt for you and certainly not a wild goose chase. Keeping your financial records organized and accessible is a good financial fitness goal for you to establish early on in your relationship. While none of us wants to think about suffering a sudden illness or an accident, it is best to be prepared so that your partner or your next of kin won't have to engage in a search-and-rescue mission if you're not able to take care of your financial obligations yourself.

THE SPECIFIC IS TERRIFIC

Okay, reverie time is up. We're now going to ask you to turn to an important task you will need to complete before you have your Financial State of the Union Meeting. We all like to keep score. We peek over at the neighbor's driveway to check out the new car they bought. We check out the furnishings in a coworker's office to measure where they stand in the food chain compared to us. It's silly and possibly counter-productive, but we can't help it. Measuring your net worth shouldn't be like that. I view it more as reading a map. You want to find out where you are on your trip to financial well-being so that you know what progress you're making and what you need to do to get to your final destination. You don't need to compare yourself to others, because they are likely on a different road headed to a different destination.

Net worth represents a snapshot of what monetary value you have amassed over your lifetime. If you and your partner decided to chuck the good life and head for Fiji today, you'd likely sell everything you have here, settle all your accounts, and take what's left to start all over in Fiji. You'd sell your house for what it's worth today. Your stock portfolio, whether up or down from what you paid for it, would fetch today's closing prices. You would pay the outstanding balance on your mortgage, not the remaining twenty-nine years' worth of payments. You'd sell the car and pay it off. You'd have a garage sale to get rid of your belongings. In sum, you'd wipe out all traces of your life here on the mainland and take the money left over and run to Fiji. What you take with you to Fiji is similar to your net worth. What all your assets are worth today, what you owe, and what's left over for you.

Taking stock of your net worth is helpful not only for knowing the absolute value but also for the process of inventorying the discards to be and treasures you've accumulated. Looking at a list of what you've worked so hard for might open your eyes to the possibility that your money could be put to different use. Maybe a reorganization or better controls are in order. So, don't just look at the bottom-line number. Really assess what you need and what you've accumulated.

That being said, measuring your net worth won't require creating an inventory of every item you possess. You won't need to tag every pair of shoes, every one of the kid's toys, or every can of soup in the pantry (unless you really enjoy those types of projects). Financial assets and big-ticket items are going to be 99 percent of your net worth, so we'll focus on those.

Begin by making a list of your financial assets—those that are cash or quickly convertible to cash. Bank accounts, piggy banks, certificates of deposit, and money market mutual funds not held in retirement accounts fall into this category. The reason they are called liquid assets is that they can be quickly converted from one "solid" state (that asset) to another (cash).

Less liquid, but still convertible to cash with little effort, are your savings and investments. These items, such as investment and retirement accounts, are assets that you've squirreled away to keep for a long time. They're not there for expenditures any more. They are the assets you've accumulated and set aside to grow and sustain you later on in life.

Lastly, you have your "tangible" assets—assets that don't exist merely in a ledger in some financial institution's computer system. These are the assets you touch every day—your home, cars, jewelry, computers, televisions, boats, and other toys. They are much less liquid and most are much more difficult to value. Do the best you can in putting a number on their value today. Not what you paid for them, not what it would cost to replace them, but what they would bring if sold as-is today. Remember the behavioral finance axiom from chapter 1 about how we value items higher if we already own them and lower if we want to buy them? Try to be conservative and fair in your valuations.

A number of resources exist for you to determine the value of your tangible assets. For example, the Kelly Blue Book is a good source to determine the approximate value of your automobile(s). You can go to www.kbb.com to determine the value range for your automobile(s) and motorcycle(s). Keep in mind that you will only be able to determine a ballpark value. Auction sites like eBay, online selling sources such as AutoTrader.com, and many others exist to assist you in determining an approximate fair market value for your goods. Simply find comparable items that are listed to get a sense of the *asking* price. What those items eventually sell for may or may not be information you can access, but with a bit of tracking persistence, you can find that out as well. Obviously, many variables exist, including geographic location, condition of the items, and so on, but for this part of your net worth assessment, an approximate value will do.

Since your home is likely to be your largest ticket item, it's important to make as accurate an assessment as you can of its value. For most of us, the value we assign our home is likely to be based on emotion as well as rational analysis. Try to avoid operating from a "sentimental value" posture. Real estate ads, your homeowner's insurance replacement value, or an appraisal can all be helpful tools for determining this value.

A NOTE FOR UNMARRIED COUPLES

For you, this process can require one additional step. Depending on your legal agreements with each other, you may have some assets separately owned and others jointly owned. Both of you may be on the line for certain debts while other debts are joint. The legalities can get very complicated, so I hope that you've documented agreements and gotten legal advice to help sort through the issues. It is worthwhile to measure individual net worth and a joint net worth separately. Going through this process and placing assets and debts into groups based on what is separately owned and what is jointly owned is a good idea. It may be eye-opening in itself and lead you to seek some legal help in determining whether the distribution represents how you want your relationship to exist.

NET WORTH WORKSHEET

With the sample sheet in Figure 4-1, you can use to determine your net worth individually and collectively. Again, resist the temptation

FIGURE 4-1. Net worth worksheet.

	Partner 1	Partner 2	Jointly Owned	Combined
Assets				
Liquid Assets				
Cash (Money Market)				
Checking Accounts				
Savings Accounts				
CDs				
Savings and Investments				
Stocks				
Bonds				
Mutual Funds				
Options				
Annuities				
Other assets in brokerage accounts				
Cash value of life insurance				
Trust funds for which you are beneficiary or you can access				
IRAs				
Vested pension benefits				
Non-marketable securities				
Ownership interest in businesses and assets				
Leases owed to you				
Loans owed to you				
Timeshares				
True collectibles				
Fixed Assets				
Home				
Other real estate				
Autos				

	Partner 1	Partner 2	Jointly Owned	Combined
Boats				
Jewelry				
Furniture				
Other machinery, equipment, and "toys"				
TOTAL ASSETS				
Liabilities				
Short Term Debt				
Charge cards				
Bank loans				
Lines of credit				
Margin debt to broker				
Salary advances				
Medical copays outstanding				
Other debt due in less than one year				
Long-Term Debt				
Mortgage				
Home equity lines				
Student loans				
Car loans				
Partnership loans or other advances				
Other debt due in more than one year				
TOTAL LIABILITIES				
TOTAL ASSETS MINUS TOTAL LIABILITIES EQUALS: NET WORTH				

to turn this into a competition with your partner. Chances are you already have a general sense of what assets each of you has brought to the marriage. Calculating your net worth will quantify that impression into cold hard numbers. Be prepared for that reality check. If you did good work during the Financial First Date, there should be no surprises here.

Are you surprised? Disappointed? Don't know what to think? For now, let's leave this at that. We'll talk a bit more about net worth and what it means in the grand scheme of things when we get to goal setting and retirement. You'll want to do some calculations to determine how long your money will last you in retirement, but for now you're done. Trust us, it will be worth the effort in the end.

MAKING A BUDGET

Remember how wonderful you felt as you left your wedding reception? The ceremony was just as you pictured it would be. People came up to you after the reception to tell you that it was the best wedding they had ever attended. The music was energizing, the food superb, and everyone was in the mood to have a wonderful time. Even the relatives you were concerned about mixing together behaved themselves. It went so well because of the planning you put into it. Left to chance, it certainly would not have been as great as it eventually was. Figuring out your financial situation and coming up with a useful plan is just as important and worthwhile. And the payoff can be greater—a lifetime of blissful financial security.

Creating a budget doesn't need to be as bad as a trip to the dentist. In fact, a trip to the dentist isn't as bad as it used to be. With today's cosmetic procedures and high-tech methods, a trip to the dentist now might be something to look forward to. Budgeting should be, too. It is just paying attention to your spending and then making some decisions about whether the way you're spending your money suits your goals. And the payoff is creating a better ability to reach those goals.

Your first step is to look upon this process with a good attitude. It's helpful, it's not a lot of work, and it's very insightful. Plus, throughout the process you'll get to use your new communications skills. Remember to go into this without a defensive or blaming mentality. The object is not to lambaste your partner about wasting money on his weekly outing with coworkers or to hide your weakness for donating to every good cause you encounter. No shame and no blame at this point.

You are merely going to keep track of all your income and expenditures for a while. Those of you using Quicken or other personal finance programs may already have such information. Those who pay for everything by automatic payment, check, or charge will also have records of all your cash flows in and out of your hands. I have some clients who have created simple spreadsheets on their personal computers to keep track of most or every expenditure they make or to balance their checkbook. Others label large manila envelopes for each category and put bills and receipts in them. Once a month they empty the envelopes and write down the results. Some of you may be used to merely glancing at your statements at the end of the month and may have automatic payment agreements with your major creditors.

This probably seems like a daunting task, but it really takes very little time. Set aside an hour or two at the beginning to set up your bookkeeping method, a few seconds every now and then to empty the receipts from your pocket, and an hour a month to record your results. These actions will reap huge benefits in the long run.

A WORD TO THE WISE

By the way, I think those automatic payment agreements are a double-edged sword. Yes, they are convenient and you avoid late payments, but in return they remove you from the process enough that you risk the possibility of really losing an awareness of where your money is going. Without physically writing the check and mailing the payment each month it's easy to lose the feeling of actually giving up money that you earned. Your cash flow process devolves into going to work, getting paid through auto deposit, paying bills through auto debits, buying everything through charge cards, and getting money out of automated teller machines when you need it. You end up feeling that the money is never really yours, there is an endless supply, and you never know how much actually belongs to you. It would be very enlightening to make all your transactions with cash for one month. Actually handing over money out of your wallet or purse is much harder than handing over a piece of plastic, and you'll think much harder about how you spend your money. I think you'll be surprised at where your money actually goes.

WHAT COMES IN/WHAT GOES OUT

Once you have all your information in hand, it's time to sit down and organize it. The objective here is to put your cash flows in and cash flows out into various categories that later will make decision making easy. Look for categories that are a combination of identifiable and meaningful. If you can't track it, there's no point in creating that category. On the other hand, just because you have details about taxes on your grocery purchases doesn't mean that it's worth tracking separately. Later on, if you find categories that seem out of whack you can drill down to the details and figure out what might be the issue.

For most of us, income is probably pretty easy to measure even if it varies in amount from month to month. Salaries and interest are usual sources of income. If you have rental property or other forms of income, include those.

Expenses should be divided into several buckets. Your mortgage and utilities goes into a housing bucket. Food is another bucket. Personal items like clothing, jewelry, and so on can be grouped together. Entertainment, charity, savings, education, and so on are all possible additional buckets.

Figure 4-2 offers an example of a budget worksheet that might work for you.

You might think of better categories or move things around depending upon your situation. Starbucks or Blockbuster or Nordstrom or Nails 'R' Us Spa or Chez McDonald's might warrant separate accounts if you suspect they might be particularly troublesome. You can add subcategories, too, if you feel that it would be helpful. Some items could fit into several categories, so maybe it's better to keep them separate. For instance, are health club dues medical or entertainment? Maybe both? Keep it separate to eliminate the temptation to justify them based on the more worthy-sounding medical reasons. I am sure you'll find some surprises once you start adding things up, but resist the urge to point out problem expenditures at this point. We're merely adding up the results and want to look at broad but meaningful groupings. Later, if tightening the belt is required, you can talk about spending details.

DURATION MATTERS

Ideally, track your expenses for a whole twelve-month period. At least have three months of representative, solid data to examine. If you're able to estimate the rest, go ahead. Remember, some expenses are seasonal or annual. For instance, utility bills may rise in the winter as you heat your house. Or, during the summer your income goes down as sales commissions shrink. Insurance pay-

FIGURE 4-2. **Family monthly budget schedule.**

	January	February	March	April
INCOME DESCRIPTION				
Wages (take-home)—partner 1	$0	$0	$0	$0
Wages (take-home)—partner 2	$0	$0	$0	$0
Interest and dividends	$0	$0	$0	$0
Miscellaneous	$0	$0	$0	$0
TOTAL INCOME	**$0**	**$0**	**$0**	**$0**
EXPENSE DESCRIPTION				
Housing				
Mortgage payment	$0	$0	$0	$0
Rent	$0	$0	$0	$0
Home repairs	$0	$0	$0	$0
Insurance	$0	$0	$0	$0
Utilities				
Electricity	$0	$0	$0	$0
Gas company	$0	$0	$0	$0
Telephone bill	$0	$0	$0	$0
Water	$0	$0	$0	$0
Cell phone	$0	$0	$0	$0
Transportation				
Auto insurance	$0	$0	$0	$0
Auto payment	$0	$0	$0	$0
Gasoline	$0	$0	$0	$0
Auto maintenance	$0	$0	$0	$0
Food				
Groceries	$0	$0	$0	$0
Necessary outside meals	$0	$0	$0	$0
Household				
Cleaning expenses	$0	$0	$0	$0
Other upkeep	$0	$0	$0	$0
Personal Care				
Beauty shop and barber	$0	$0	$0	$0
Clothing	$0	$0	$0	$0
Laundry and dry cleaning	$0	$0	$0	$0
Children				
Tuition	$0	$0	$0	$0
Child care	$0	$0	$0	$0
School supplies	$0	$0	$0	$0
Entertainment and recreation				
Cable television	$0	$0	$0	$0
Internet access	$0	$0	$0	$0

	January	February	March	April
Club dues	$0	$0	$0	$0
Subscriptions	$0	$0	$0	$0
Movie rentals	$0	$0	$0	$0
Games	$0	$0	$0	$0
Activities	$0	$0	$0	$0
Restaurants	$0	$0	$0	$0
Vacations	$0	$0	$0	$0
Health				
Health insurance	$0	$0	$0	$0
Life insurance	$0	$0	$0	$0
Medical and dental out-of-pocket	$0	$0	$0	$0
Charity	$0	$0	$0	$0
Gifts	$0	$0	$0	$0
Debt payments				
Home equity	$0	$0	$0	$0
Credit card payments	$0	$0	$0	$0
Other debt payments	$0	$0	$0	$0
Miscellaneous	$0	$0	$0	$0
TOTAL EXPENSES	**$0**	**$0**	**$0**	**$0**
CASH (SHORT) EXTRA	**$0**	**$0**	**$0**	**$0**

ments, dues, and such are usually annual or biannual, so be sure to factor them in. Vacations are not usually consistent in timing or expense, so they also need to be included and carefully measured. Gifts, 401(k), and IRA contributions, and charitable giving are not usually monthly items, so keep them in mind.

Once you have all this put together, it's easiest to think about the results in monthly terms. Divide the dollar amounts by the number of months you've accumulated to get the monthly average. If you're really ambitious, then divide each monthly average expense amount into your average monthly total income. This will tell you what percentage of your income you spent on each of the categories. You'll see, for instance, that you spent 25 percent of your income on food for your cat Fluffy (if that's the case, maybe Fluffy needs a more fitting name).

FOR COMPARISON PURPOSES

Figure 4-3 shows the average budget of the American family in 2004 as compiled from a diary kept by about 100,000 households for the Bureau of Labor Statistics. This data represents averages, but it can also be cut by various economic, geographic, and demographic categories to get a more representative comparison with your situation.

"Average" is a very elusive term. Keep in mind what Mark Twain said about numbers (though he was actually quoting Benjamin Disraeli) when he wrote, "There are lies, damned lies, and statistics." Everyone's family expenditures will vary, but it's important to look at these numbers in case you discover serious discrepancies between your spending habits and those of the average American family. Obviously, if you live in some place like the Bay Area in and around San Francisco or in Manhattan, your housing costs are going to be higher and that may skew your comparison. Keep in mind that average doesn't mean "ideal." Don't try to trim your budget or expenses to match these numbers.

AT LAST, THE MEETING BEGINS

At the end of your first date, you set up a time and a place for this meeting, you did your net worth and budget homework in preparation for the meeting, and now it's time to really get down to business. The purpose of this meeting is to assess where you have been, where you are now, and to decide together where you want to go next. All of the previous guidelines about communication still apply. This meeting might generate more emotional heat than the previous one, and you may need to take breaks when feelings rise. That's to be expected, and in some ways welcome. A false consensus, both of you agreeing just to agree, isn't going to prove fruitful

FIGURE 4-3. **2004 expenditures as percentage of after-tax take-home pay.**

Savings	**17.0%**
Food at home	**6.4%**
Food away from home	**4.7%**
Alcoholic beverages	**0.9%**
Tobacco products and smoking supplies	**0.6%**
Housing	**26.6%**
Shelter	15.3%
Utilities, fuels, and public services	5.6%
Natural gas	0.8%
Electricity	2.0%
Fuel oil and other fuels	0.2%
Telephone services	1.9%
Water and other public services	0.6%
Household operations	1.4%
Personal services	0.6%
Other household expenses	0.9%
Housekeeping supplies	1.1%
Laundry and cleaning supplies	0.3%
Other household products	0.6%
Postage and stationery	0.3%
Household furnishings and equipment	3.1%
Apparel and services	3.5%
Transportation	**14.9%**
Vehicle purchases (net outlay)	6.5%
Gasoline and motor oil	3.1%
Other vehicle expenses	4.5%
Vehicle finance charges	0.6%
Maintenance and repairs	1.2%
Vehicle insurance	1.8%
Vehicle rental, leases, licenses, other charges	0.8%
Public transportation	0.8%
Health care	**4.9%**
Health insurance	2.5%
Medical services	1.2%
Drugs	0.9%
Medical supplies	0.2%
Entertainment	**4.2%**
Fees and admissions	1.0%
Television, radios, sound equipment	1.5%
Pets, toys, hobbies, and playground equipment	0.7%
Other entertainment supplies, equipment, and services	1.0%
Personal care products and services	**1.1%**

(continues)

FIGURE 4-3. **Continued.**

Reading	**0.2%**
Education	**1.7%**
Miscellaneous	**1.3%**
Charity	**2.7%**
Personal insurance and pensions	**9.2%**
Life and other personal insurance	0.7%
Pensions and Social Security	8.5%

Source: U.S. Bureau of Labor Statistics, "Consumer Expenditure Survey" (www.bls.gov).

over the long haul. Open, honest, and at times, heated exchanges of viewpoint, values, and vision are to be expected and welcome.

First, it's a good idea to look at your budget results. Remember, the point of this exercise is not to make drastic across-the-board cuts or blame and criticize either yourself or your partner. You both need to examine where your money is going and determine whether it is going where it best meets your life goals and needs. Do some soul-searching and some negotiation with your partner to figure out what can be cut and where it should go. Money spent on cigarettes and coffee may be an unneeded luxury for one partner but may be a necessity for another. Weigh the trade-offs of various categories.

Look for places to downsize that have the least impact on your lifestyle. A club membership that rarely gets used could be eliminated or downsized. That big sport-utility vehicle that you used to use to haul the kids around might not be required now that they've reached the age when they rarely go anywhere with mom and dad anyway. Save money with coupons or off-season purchases.

Don't just focus on the dubious items that come up. Now might be a good time to look at some of your ongoing expenses and look for ways to economize that won't drastically change your lifestyle. For example, review your insurance policies to look for ways to save.

BEWARE THE BUDGET BUSTER

A budget buster is using credit cards for necessities. Credit card companies have done studies and found that users spend at least

30 percent more when they use a card. You might feel funny just charging a $10 item, so you put a few more items in your basket, or you don't shop around as aggressively because you aren't reaching in your pocket for the money. You focus on the convenience or the difference in the monthly payment rather than the true cost. Carry some cash with you and get in the habit of using it for those miscellaneous purchases. I bet you don't feel as willing to look for those other items to put in your shopping basket. And who knows, that five dollars you kept in your wallet may be the start of a fund you're going to establish to finance your children's college education.

GOAL SETTING

Here we are at last. The crux of the matter. The yolk of the egg. The proof in the pudding.

This is the moment in the meeting when we finally get an answer to, "You're probably wondering why I asked all of you to join me here today."

I'm fairly certain that as a couple, you've shared your vision of what you think your life together will be like. You probably spent countless hours in contemplation of that vision. How much of that vision you shared with your partner depends a lot upon personality and circumstance. For most of you, those goals may have remained nebulous desires floating in a sea of possibilities not anchored to any real dates or specific plans of action. That's about to end. Those other goals just as easily could have been called "dreams." They share many of the same ethereal qualities of a dream. What you're here to discuss is reality. Hard Truths. Action Plans. Due Dates.

I suppose it is at this point especially that our State of the Union metaphor really breaks down. This is not the time for grand, general pronouncements about reforming education in this country. This is a time for taking specific, manageable, daily, weekly, and monthly steps toward a tangible, attainable goal like reducing credit card debt to zero in two years. Because you want to make certain that your goals aren't pie-in-the-sky platitudes (can pie be served on a platitude?), you have to:

- Be Specific

- Be Realistic

- Think Action-Oriented

- Account for Dual Accountability

- Have Consequences and Rewards for Not Meeting or Meeting Deadlines

- Prioritize Wisely

Obviously, most of you realize that it's not enough to just say that you want to get out of debt or save more money this year. That's why specific goals are important. In fact, I think that being specific is so important, that I prefer not to use the term goal; instead, I'd like you to refer to each of the commitments you make together as a couple as *action plans*. Why? Because the two words together tell you all you need to know. You are going to take action(s) and you are going to formulate a plan to make certain that action gets accomplished. Sounds simple, right?

Let's see an action plan in action. Robert and Kathy Simpson have been married for the last seven years. They have a daughter, Sarah, who just turned four. The couple both work, Robert as a first assistant camera operator, with designs on one day being a cinematographer, and Kathy as a publicist for a studio. Robert's work is by nature sporadic. He either is working eighteen hour days on location or in the studio for three months at a time, or he is sitting at home recuperating for a few weeks before the next film project comes along. With all his overtime, he has averaged $85,000 a year in salary for the last three years. Kathy earns $45,000. Their combined income of $130,000 affords them a fairly nice lifestyle. Right now, their net worth, thanks to some stocks and the equity in their home is a more than respectable (for a couple in their early thirties) $225,000.

In terms of budget, they are doing fairly well. They both have a car payment that they take care of individually from their own paycheck. Their credit card debt is a real variable. It goes up mostly when Robert has to buy new equipment for work. While they are a deductible business/tax expense, the items are expensive. They both contribute to paying off the cards as soon as possible, but when Robert is working, he has little time left over for doing much of anything, so financial decisions fall on Kathy's shoulders. She tries to make reasonable decisions, but gets flustered when, without warning, she finds a $3,000 to $5,000 surprise on the Visa bill. Those kinds of surprises make budgeting tough, and they've made a commitment to have Robert turn over receipts immediately, and not when he's in decompression mode.

Following their Financial State of the Union Meeting. They set three high-priority goals—one short term, one medium term, and one long term.

1. Short term: Pay down credit card debt of $7,345 in the next three months.

2. Medium term: Increase monthly cushion from three months to six monts.

3. Long term: Establish a college tuition savings plan that will yield them $60,000 dollars in thirteen years.

Figure 4-4 takes a look at an action plan the two of them put together to reach their medium-term goal within one year.

On paper, this looks like a fairly straightforward endeavor. The two of them sat down to review their finances, saw a shortfall they wanted to address, and then planned on how to meet that goal. Well, by looking at the action plan you can see how they worked their way through the process to arrive at a monthly dollar figure

FIGURE 4-4.   Cushion increase action plan.

Total Monthly Expenses	$4,388
Current Savings	$13,565
Savings Target	$27,000
Target Date of Completion	5/15/07
Number of Months to Target	12
Present Savings/Month	$875
Amount Needed to Save	$13,435
Savings/Month to Reach Target	$1,119.58
Target Savings Increase	$244.58

Specific Action Plan	Agent	Savings	
Pack lunch instead of buy on site twice a week	Robert	$60/month	Action Taken
Reduce manicure/pedicure to bi-monthly visits	Kathy	$40/month	Action Taken
Quit smoking cigars	Robert	$60/month	Action Taken
Cancel Laundry Service	Robert/Kathy	$100/month	Action Taken
Total Monthly Savings		**$260.00**	

they needed to save in the next twelve-month period. What you don't see is the kind of give and take that had to transpire between the two of them before they could agree on the best plan of action. While it may be obvious, let's lay some cards on the table. Robert is a bit of a Ritz-Carlton. He definitely enjoys the finer things in life, and not just cigars. His belief is that if you're going to buy something, it makes sense to buy the best—whether it's a pair of sunglasses, a tape measure for work, or a piece of expensive gear for his job. Kathy is close to an Econo Lodger but with a few exceptions. She loves her creature comforts and believes that it's important psychologically that she pamper herself just a bit—she works hard and mothering Sarah is a challenge, she needs some relief from her stress. It could be worse—she doesn't drink, take drugs, or spend wildly.

So, when it came time to figure out what they could cut back on, the two of them had to undertake some steps to negotiate an agreement they could both sign off on. For Robert, his choices of what to cut back on came down to two things he held near and dear to him—cigars and golfing. Robert and his usual crew from the set, when they aren't working, enjoy their downtime by golfing. It's an expensive hobby. Greens fees average $80.00 for eighteen holes, his clubs cost him $1,200.00, and the after-golf drinks and dinner can easily run to $100.00. That doesn't include the cigars, which are an intimate part of the ritual. Kathy would have preferred he give up the golfing, but Robert let her know that those golf outings were a necessary part of his team building with his crew and also led to more work. More importantly, they provided him with much-needed stress relief. Although it was a tough call, the cigars were out. Similar kinds of negotiating went on to reach their goal amount. They had to work their way through a complex nexus of emotion, desire, prioritizing, and urging and compromising to get there.

In the next part of the book, we'll take a more detailed look at the finances and backgrounds of couples as they pursue other financial action plans. For now, let this example suffice as a lesson in how the process works on even this most elementary of levels.

Big or small, high priority or low priority, short term or long term, any of your action plans/goals need to be treated in much the same way. The process remains much the same. Note that on the action plan above, Robert and Kathy monitor their success/failure at accomplishing each substep on a weekly basis, thus ensuring that they are holding themselves accountable for their success. With mutually agreed-upon goals, both of them work on meeting their goals together. Remember: It is not enough to simply identify your goals. The most important next step is to determine a way that you can afford whatever is on your list of goals.

One of the reasons that Robert and Kathy chose this middle-term goal is because in my meetings with them, I urged them to have a six-month cushion. That cushion is a fund that will pay for all their expenses for a six-month period. This is especially important since Robert's work isn't a guaranteed income. I urge all my clients to have that kind of cushion. None of us wants to think that we can lose our job, become temporarily disabled, or otherwise not able to contribute financially. With a little sacrifice and planning they were able to find the money in their budget to achieve their goal. In fact, I have a lot of movie and television celebrities who may go for years without working—cushion planning is crucial for them.

There are, of course, other eventualities in life that we can predict and plan for. In the second half of this book, we will take a look at many of them including: home purchase, starting/expanding your family, financing education, and retiring. In doing so, we'll show you how various couples managed to negotiate the terms of their agreements, working together despite the differences in their financial styles, their differing views on the utility of money, relative risk aversion, and decision-making skills. We will truly be putting it all together to show how open communication, fundamental financial knowledge, and a firm commitment can transform your financial life and lead you to bliss.

MERGING AND MANAGING YOUR FINANCIAL LIFE TOGETHER

CHAPTER 5

YOURS, MINE, AND OURS

Marrying Your Finances . . . Or Not

Those of you reading this who are parents probably understand this better than most: Sharing is hard. It's a difficult concept to teach our children and remains a difficult concept for us as adults. Whether it's because we retain some genetic hard-wiring that insists we stock up for the inevitable famine/downturn that could threaten our existence or we are less Darwinian than that, couplehood both suits our strengths and cuts against our grain. When we enter into couplehood, we bring with us assumptions about the form our union will take. I hope that in your various discussions up to this point, this issue (the yours, mine, ours dilemma as I call it) has emerged. If it hasn't yet, then you certainly need to bring it out into the open. Whether you choose, or are able to enter into, a legally recognized union, or engage in some other type of merging of lives and finances, you need to address some fundamental questions.

I've noticed that couples who come to me for financial advice fall into several fairly defined categories when it comes to their feelings about what kind of financial union they are entering into. I love the fifty-fiftyers. I just do. They are the idealists, the ones who believe that a marriage is a true union of equals. What was once yours is now mine, and what was once mine is now yours. Or, more simply, there's no longer any yours and mine but only and exclusively an "OURS." Assets, liabilities, inheritances, salaries, stock holdings, and so on, are now mingled together in one pool that dissolves whatever boundaries may have existed before. Just like when you pour one glass of water into another, it becomes impossible to identify the source of one molecule or another, so too are the finances of the fifty-fiftyers.

CALL ME A SKEPTIC, BUT . . .

Of course, we are talking about human beings here, so I'm a bit skeptical whenever I encounter the blissfully joined fifty-fiftyer. Their point of view is wonderful, especially if they pair off with another of their kind. That doesn't always happen in the real world. The worst-case scenario is if they hook up with a "me, myself, and I" type. Now, don't get too high and mighty here and look down your nose at what you presume to be selfish oafs who tromp among the fifty-fiftyers' carefully cultivated daisy patches plucking petals and saying, "I love me. I love me not? Fughetaboudit! Of course I love me!"

Characteristics of the me, myself, and I type lurk within every one of us. I doubt that any fifty-fiftyer goes through life without ever checking the scorecard to see to whom those contributions to the collective bottom line can be attributed. The inverse is also true—just because you are a me, myself, and I type and want credit where credit is due for your contributions, that doesn't mean that you can't or won't contribute to the collective. You just want to make certain that a tally is kept and when the rewards are divvied up, or if the union should be dissolved somehow, that you receive in equal measure to what you gave. Is that so wrong? If these people were baseball players, they'd likely be the pitchers on the team. Sure, they can be team players, and they want to win, but they are comfortable with the idea that in the box score at the end of the game, they will be the only ones who are actually given credit for a "W"—a win, or an "L"—for a loss. They're willing to be stand-up guys and gals and accept that kind of responsibility. Sure, their individual statistics are important to them too, but their individual success also helps to drive the team's success.

A HAPPY MEDIUM?

Somewhere in the middle between these opposite ends of the spectrum lie the accomodationists. They pay a kind of lip service to the communist ideal of a shared collective, but they know that true sharing isn't really practical or productive. They're not so concerned about keeping score officially and wanting their finances kept separate as the me, myself, and I types; they just want to lie low and enjoy the fruitful benefits of the union. Just don't send too many party officials around to make sure that the books are in order or who are in need of a bribe. These individuals take a somewhat laissez-faire attitude toward the financial union. They were happy before the takeover, they can accommodate whatever the new regime has in mind, but basically they are going to go along to get along. But don't be fooled by their accommodating nature. Somewhere within them the me, myself, and I characteristics lie dormant. Under the right set of circumstances, the less positive aspect of that type can burst out and subvert any of the carefully laid plans of the other two types. You'll have to pick up on subtle cues from this type to determine just how strong their underlying tendencies are—you may think they are amenable to the fifty-fifty-ers egalitarian principles, but then one day you discover a savings account, an investment fund, or some other previously undisclosed bit of income they'd forgotten about. They're not bad people; they just struggle with financial intimacy issues.

A REALITY CHECK

In truth, we are all accomodationists to a certain extent. On the outside we may be nodding and agreeing, but on the inside we are agitated at the thought but unwilling to bare our souls and fight openly. Sometimes avoiding conflict seems the easier way to go, but surviving to fight another day presupposes a couple of things—you will have to fight that battle sometime, and you don't think you're arguments are strong enough to win.

That's not to say that the accomodationists are all bad. Being flexible and willing to compromise are admirable traits—especially when they are motivated by empathy and not evasion. Accomodationists tend to be empathetic and walk miles in other people's shoes. The hope is that after a long trial run, they will develop a firm allegiance to the cause and settle firmly in their position. I know a lot of couples who have gone through a divorce or separation. When it came time for the financials to be settled, they came to me and said, "My God. I can't believe how much my ex has changed. I never knew he/she felt this way. I feel betrayed. How could I have been so wrong?" Chances are we're talking about an accomodationist showing his or her true colors under duress.

Chances are if you have the kinds of conversations that we've suggested, you won't end up being surprised down the road. That's the key. Any of the three types that I mentioned can get along and can come to terms with how they want to handle their finances. As long you go into the agreement knowing what you're going to get, you can allow for it (that's the positive accomodationist trait shining through), adapt to it, and accept it. As time and circumstances change, you may find your position shifting—for instance, if you inherit a great deal of money, win the lottery, have an unanticipated boost in salary or bonus. You may decide after a period of time that how you handle the yours, mine, ours, issue needs to be revisited. Do so. Do so openly and honestly. That's what I did.

MY STORY

My husband I are a good example of two people with fairly divergent financial situations. I used to be employed by a major investment firm. He has long been established in his medical practice. We used to keep our finances jointly. We'd even sit down each month and go over the bills and pay them together. In time, and because my circumstances changed, keeping our accounts separate made more sense. As I moved into owning my own business it became apparent that we needed to change some of our procedures. Neither of us enjoyed going over all the expenditures I had in order to get my business up and running. I didn't feel like justifying the cost of my expensive custom-made furniture for the office, and he didn't like hearing the justification. So, now he has his accounts and I have mine, and we have ours. As has been true with most issues in this book, there are multiple solutions to every problem. How you decide and what you decide is a matter of personal preference. What works for my husband and me may not work for you and vice versa.

The fundamental truth underlying this entire book remains: The unexamined financial life will not lead to bliss. While it is tempting to experience the near-Nirvana of temporary complete agreement, that Nirvana is exactly what I said—near and temporary. Better to face all of these questions and resolve to the best of your ability and experience each of these issues. Deciding what is yours, mine, and ours, is a crucial preparatory step to dealing with the major life and financial issues that we present in the remainder of this chapter. As always honesty is the best policy.

ANOTHER SOBERING REALITY

Although in retrospect I realize now that I shouldn't have been stunned by this, that was my reaction when I watched a recent *Oprah!* in which many women confessed to stealing money from their husband's wallets—in addition to other kinds of financial "cheating." I'm sure that a like number of men have done the same thing to their partners. An entire complex of reasons exists why I should not have been surprised by these actions. We live in a culture in which sexual infidelity is an everyday occurrence. Financial infidelity isn't something we often talk about, and it may be just one of many other dirty little secrets that we keep. How we conduct our financial lives is no different, has the same antecedents in our past, and is as complicated as the interplay of heredity and environment that shapes our personality. Although I've just given you three more "categories" of financial types, reality is never that cut-and-dry. Please keep that in mind as you and your partner sort out how you are going to handle your financial life together. Firm, flexible, and fair are about as good a set of guidelines as any that I can provide for you as you enter into this next negotiation as a couple.

Statistics are not available to support a contention that a particular choice (joint versus separate accounts) is the "best" or the "most popular." As you negotiate these decisions, keep this in mind. Some couples find that it is easier for each person to be responsible for covering certain bills: You take the mortgage, car payment, and utilities and I'll cover the groceries, gas, and incidentals. Some may take the approach that (and Data Darlings seem to love this idea) you contribute X percent each month, therefore you pay X percent of the total expenses for the month. Who is responsible for physically paying the bills can be divvied up as well in a similar fashion. No matter how you decide or what you decide, make sure that the arrangement is one you both can live with. As we suggested in the budgeting section, it is probably a good idea to try out the who pays/who sends arrangement on a trial basis of a month or more. If it works for both parties, keep on that track. If it doesn't, then come up with another arrangement.

Obviously, you want to avoid the one person pays–one person spends scenario, particularly if the person responsible for doing both doesn't have the time or inclination to keep the other partner apprised of what is going on. I can't stress enough how important it is for both partners to know what's going on financially. I hate to say this, but I have seen a number of examples of couples in which one partner prefers to remain completely in the dark about the financial operations of their joint enterprise.

DIVIDE, DUET/DIVVY, DECIDE, AND DO

No, that's not the name of the law firm that represents me, that's the alliterative lineup of issues to consider when you merge finances with another person. Whether married or not, one of the biggest stumbling blocks I've seen is if assets coming into the relationship are unequal or if income is unequal. That's a pretty common experience. What's the likelihood that you and your partner are going to have a net worth with seats next to one another—in the same ball park maybe, but not that close. So regardless of the income divide that separates you, you've got some decisions to make.

- Do you split living expenses fifty-fifty no matter what, or do you split them relative to income?

- How much say does one partner have over how the other spends his or her money?

- Who makes the investment decisions?

- Do you pool your money or keep separate accounts and a third account for expenses?

- Does one of you become the bookkeeper/accountant?

I've seen relationships work with all of the various permutations of these issues. And I've seen them collapse. The key really is not which decision to make but making a choice based upon honest communication and caring. Don't ignore your concerns for your financial security and grudgingly give in because you feel you're dealing from a weaker position. Make sure your concerns are heard and dealt with in some way. You might not get everything you want, but some compromise or alternative may address your needs. And be sure to reciprocate. All the keys to communicating effectively we learned in previous chapters need to continue for all the other issues that arise throughout your life together.

COMPROMISING POSITIONS

I want to add a note here about compromise. In my experience, couples have a very different view of what that concept means in practical application. I don't know who expressed this idea first, but I've heard it said that a compromise creates a situation in which both parties walk away unhappy—neither of them getting exactly what they want. I've seen some couples avoid this by coming up with a compromised version of what most people think of as a true compromise. They avoided the whole negotiation process by agreeing that they would take turns. Whenever there was a financial issue that needed resolution, Partner A would get her way. The next occurrence, Partner B got her way. I don't agree with this way of doing things, but, again, the point here is that this couple worked out a method that worked for them. While their solution didn't live up to the letter of the definition, and communication experts and some psychologists may say that they didn't decide at all—but isn't choosing not to decide a decision?—the system worked for them. That's the key. Shut the door on the critics who tell you that your system doesn't work.

Maybe in the ideal world it is possible to have a true marriage of two minds that admits no impediments, but you'd have a hard time coming up with a real-world example of how that works all the time every time. I'm not suggesting that you abandon all hope of achieving some kind of understanding with your partner and resort to coin-tossing, die-rolling, or straw-drawing methods for arriving at decisions. What I am saying is that with a little planning and organization you can eliminate time pressure as one of the forces at work pushing you toward one of those methods. As much as I entreat you to be kind and considerate, I want to add to that list—be realistic. Perfect harmony and the ultimate compromise may be beyond your reach. Aim high, but recognize that your aim may exceed your reach.

NO SECRETS

Keeping and Maintaining Good Financial Records

Your three-hour cruise with a fishing buddy turns into a three-year version of the movie *Castaway*. Despite the passing months with no sign of you or your boat, your partner never gives up hope for your return. She handles things as best she can, but the lost income forces her to take drastic measures. She has had to use what little liquid assets she could scrounge up. In order to pay the bills, she has had to sell her treasured collection of beer tap handles that the two of you had spent decades and countless frequent flier miles amassing. Worse yet, the buyer was a despised fellow collector who was way too competitive about collecting and always needed to best you. Miraculously, a group trying to locate Amelia Earhart's plane stumbles across you on some deserted island and you return home to tons of publicity. After an emotional greeting, your partner explains what she has had to do to keep you financially afloat. You respond by saying that you had taken out a long-term disability insurance policy several years ago, and it would have paid enough monthly to sustain her through all of this. Unfortunately, you forgot to tell your partner about the policy. As a result, you've lost your prized collection and all those memories for no reason. And to your arch-nemesis. Be prepared to get sent back to your deserted island!

MEANWHILE, BACK AT THE REALITY HOTEL

Neither death nor disability are pleasant to think about (the same is true of divorce or dissolution of your union) but you can't avoid them forever. Many of us have dealt with the death of a parent or spouse, and we've gone through the traumatic experience of sorting through a lifetime of documents to figure out how to settle things for our loved one. It can be difficult enough because of our grieving, but missing and disorganized information makes it even more stressful than it should be. Assets might go unclaimed and benefits due our heirs might be unknown because of the lack of information. Emotions run high during a divorce proceeding or when you have decided to end your couplehood. You don't need the added stress and complication of compiling this information.

In the concluding section of this chapter, we'll go over the documents and information you'll need to keep track of, share with your partner, and keep in a safe, centralized location. Managing this information and sharing it with your partner will ensure that your partner can run things if you should become disabled and will ensure that at your death the estate you worked so hard to create over your lifetime will remain intact and be handled in the way you want. It's also a very good idea that the two of you share the location of these documents with your children, siblings, and parents. In fact, I believe so strongly in keeping these records in a safe, secure place,

I provide each of my clients with a handsome wooden box for re-cord storage.

This is no time for secrets. The revelation of an estranged off-spring or an offshore account can have a large impact upon your care and your survivors.

SO, YOU THOUGHT YOU WERE GOING TO PULL A FAST ONE . . .

The last section of this list gives a laundry list of agreements that unmarried couples might enter into. At first, many couples may choose not to enter into a legal union because they don't like the constraints implicit in a union sanctioned by the state government. They may not feel that their union needs the blessing of any outside agency. The truth is that whether you marry or not (particularly if you are a heterosexual couple) the state already has some legal accommodations in place that you may have to encounter, espe-cially if the union dissolves. That's where things can get particularly tricky for nonmarried couples. Married partners have more estab-lished rights and processes for dealing with disability and survival issues. As you well know, state laws are all over the place regarding the rights of surviving partners and even surviving children of un-married couples. Laws vary from state to state and even within a single state the laws are inconsistent. It is important for tax and legal reasons that these documents establish your agreements re-garding ownership and other issues.

Again, unlike those decrees that affect a marriage, there is really no consistent default decree for unmarried couples in these situations. You need to delineate how your agreement with your partner was handled and should be handled at your death or dis-ability. If you have previous unmarried partners, the documents from those relationships should be included. If agreements were not written down, a thorough description of the understandings or oral agreements is necessary, especially if there is a chance that an heir or former partner would have a claim to your estate. We will take a look at some of these issues in more detail in the next chapter when we deal with specific life events that occur in the history of all couples. For now, keep in mind that preparedness is the best course of action regardless of the legal status of your partnership.

Regardless of that legal status, many of these documents also require some explanation or further information. It's helpful to have access to the documents, but it's even more important to know what to do with them. It is essential to have an inventory of all the documents listing the necessary information that makes them accessible. For instance, retirement accounts would need to list beneficiaries and bank accounts should list any cosigners or co-owners.

Where do you keep all this information and who has access? On your computer? In a safe-deposit box? With your lawyer? In a secret compartment in your basement? Some people prefer safe-deposit boxes for originals, but please be sure that the people who will need access to the documents also have access to your safe-deposit box.

Ideally, the more people who have access to the information the better. Relying on one person, especially your partner, doesn't cover all contingencies. What if you both are in a car crash? Who will have access to the necessary information to make decisions on your behalf and keep things running? A parent, child, sibling, lawyer, or other trusted individual should have copies of your information or at least access to it. More than one person should have access to the whole picture, but if you're concerned about having more people know so much about you, it's possible to set up a sort of tiered system. Give certain people access to the information needed if you're disabled and others the information required if you die. Another person might have access to relationship-related or business-related documents. But make sure that more than one person knows where to find the complete set of information.

General
    Name
    Address
    Aliases
    Veteran service information
    Parents' information
Children
Spouses
Other important people
Financial (names, amounts, account numbers, who to contact)
    Bank
        Accounts
        Safe-deposit boxes
        Payable-on-death bank accounts
    Brokerage accounts
    Insurance
    401(k)
    Trusts
    Retirement plans and pensions
Government Benefits
Financial Obligations
    Car
    Mortgage
    Leases/rental agreements
    Credit cards
    Promissory notes
    Alimony
    Support
    Lawsuits and settlements
Employment
Memberships

Small Business
    Name

Lawyer
Accountant
Medical Information
    Doctors
    Insurance
    Living will or other health-care directive
Death-Related Instructions
    Will and any codicils
    Announcement
    Service
    Burial/cremation
    Organ donation
    Other donations
    Other requests
Day-to-Day Living
    Contracts with service providers
    Instructions for keeping the household running (unique
    issues)
    Animal care
Secured Places and Passwords
Legal Documents
    Birth certificate
    Social Security card
    Passport
    Power of attorney
    Military discharge
    Marriage certificate
    Prenuptial agreements
    Postnuptial agreements
    Name change documents
    Divorce papers
    Other legal documents/court orders, and so on
Relationship-Related Documents
    Living-together contract

Property agreements and contracts
Contract for ownership interests in a house (or other specified property)
Agreement to keep property separate
Agreement on shared property
List of jointly owned property
Agreement for a joint purchase
Ownership transfer documents
Agreement covering homemaking services
Acknowledgement of parenthood

As you can see, this is a fairly exhaustive list, and you could potentially exhaust yourself in the process of pulling all of this information together at the time of, or in the wake of, a crisis. This is also not the time when you want to have your partner be surprised by any interesting revelations about your past—personal or financial. Full disclosure is still the best option. An annual or biannual review of these documents is also a good idea. As your life changes, this information will change, and it's a good idea to update the keeper of the information as soon as anything changes. A few minutes of review and preparation now can save countless hours of headache down the line.

SUCCESSFULLY
PREPARING FOR YOUR
FINANCIAL LIFE EVENTS

SETTING UP HOUSE

I don't know about you, but on the one hand I love surprises—pleasant ones, that is. On the other hand, I hate not being prepared for something. Part of my desire to always be prepared is that I am the product of two people who had Depression-era parents. If you're a Baby Boomer than you know what I mean. My mother was close to being one of those wear-clean-underwear-have-a-quarter-with-you-for-a-phone-call-worst-case-scenario-better-save-it-for-a-rainy-day kinds of women who we all sometimes mock—that is, until the rainy day when you're meeting her for lunch and you look like you've just stepped off the set of Titanic and she's sitting there dry as the Sahara. You sheepishly thank her for the mini-brella she always keeps in her purse just in case. You're not sure what the just in case could be—her normal umbrella is the size of Madison Square Garden and appears to be constructed of the same materials.

My husband's parents and others like them learned well several lessons. They were savers. They avoided credit card debt like it was the plague—and in many ways it is. They thought long term and not short term. If they couldn't afford it, they'd wait until they could. They didn't mortgage themselves up to their eyeballs. While they may not have always appeared to really enjoy life to the fullest, they were determined to get to retirement and beyond and remain financially solvent, independent, and certain they would be able to pass something along to the next generation. So, for me at least, it was worth putting up with some of the overly cautious stuff.

Now it's my turn to be the Nervous Nellie in your life. I know that some of the material in this chapter is going to come across as doom and gloom at worst and cautious at best. That's okay. I'm trying to make a point here about how taking up permanent residence in the Reality Hotel is probably a good thing—not that I don't advocate occasional side trips and week-long ventures outside it. Buying a home, starting or expanding your family, retiring all should be joyous events in your life. And they can be if you plan carefully for them. I want you jumping up and down for joy and not grasping for the straws that flutter in the turbulent wake of opportunities nearly lost.

There are planners and there are the rest of us. My hope is for all of the couples reading this book that at least one of you is a planner. If you don't have one don't despair. In this chapter we are going to look at the major life events that any couple is likely to experience—from buying a home to having children to retiring and more, we've got your bases covered. The pace of life is so great these days that even these milestones can sneak up on you if you aren't careful. More important, the costs associated with these life events have risen to such heights that the play-it-by-ear attitude that once meant you could still get by now means that you could take it in the ear and suffer harsh consequences. Nobody wants that kind of surprise.

I DO OR NOT I DO

It used to be such a simple decision. You met, fell in love with each other, and are committed to each other so you marry. You had 2.5

kids, bought the house with the white picket fence, and got the gold watch when you retired from the company for which you worked for forty-five years. Then you and your blushing bride of equal duration settled into retirement. A lot has changed. Over time, remaining unmarried became an attractive alternative to some couples who wanted a trial run before deciding whether marriage would work for them. Now, remaining unmarried has become a solution for even more situations, from couples contemplating marriage to seniors not wanting to risk their estates or their social security benefits, from divorced people who aren't willing to accept the emotional or financial risk of marriage again to same-sex couples who really want to be legally married but are not allowed.

Some people choose to live together just for the companionship or help with finances, such as struggling graduate students or single mothers who band together to help each other. In all, the 2000 Census counted 5.4 million unmarried couples living together—a 72 percent increase since 1990. If you are one of these unmarried couples, just think of the debate that went on figuring out how to introduce your (pick one—boyfriend/girlfriend, special friend, partner, significant other, roommate, lover). I sincerely doubt that POSSLQ (person of the opposite sex sharing living quarters—the Census Bureau's definition) entered the debate but in these enlightened times who knows? What I do know is that all these nom de union choices are an indication of all the various complications and decisions facing you.

Marriage affords many positive legal and financial benefits that unmarried couples have to work a little harder to achieve. But, for the most part, they are achievable with some planning and effort. Many of the issues are well beyond the scope of this book. We'll try to point out the main issues, but answers to legal and financial issues require experts who can examine all the aspects of your relationship and your unique needs to assist you as you form your version of couplehood.

THE CONTRACTUAL BASIS OF MARRIAGE

The reason why financial matters are a relatively straight-forward part of marriage is that married persons enter into a contract with well-established, although probably not so well-known, legal ramifications, particularly pertaining to property rights. Unmarried couples, however, aren't governed by those rules. They are free to establish their own set of guidelines. In the absence of any guidelines, they are treated by the law just as if they were any set of strangers entering into any other legal brawl.

Living together, in and of itself, does not create a contractual relationship. It also doesn't entitle either party to a property settlement should you split up or one of you die. As a result, all the furniture you bought together, all the rent one of you paid for the other, and your commingled assets are divided based on established contract law rather than on your informal understandings. If you signed the lease, you are liable even if you move out. If your partner's name is on the car title it belongs to her even though you drove it and contributed to the purchase, upkeep, and insuring of it. I cannot stress enough how important it is for unmarried couples to write down contracts to clarify their wishes regarding property rights and to take actions to keep property rights consistent with the contracts. In this case, if you don't clearly spell out the terms of your arrangement, you may end up being surprised by how the courts resolve matters should you and your partner part ways. The old adage about an ounce of prevention couldn't be more apt. In this case, a few sheets of paper are worth more than the reams of aggravation you're likely to encounter down the line.

Ever wonder why the prenuptial agreement became a necessity? It's because the law is much more straightforward in its treatment of property and marital assets. If you and your partner want to enter into an agreement that is not standard issue, the prenup is the way to go. This is another reason why it's important to enter into the marriage clear-eyed and clear-minded. That's also why it's not just a legal instrument for Hollywood's elite. As unromantic as it may sound, before you say, "I do" on your wedding day, it's a good idea to have the kinds of talks we suggest that married couples have.

All that being said, whether married or not, the emotional issues likely are a larger issue than the financial matters when establishing a relationship. Trust and commitment are essential ingredients in a relationship, and the two of you need to use another essential ingredient—communication—to work through these financial and legal issues so that trust and commitment remain strong. Only the two of you can decide whether adding your partner to the title of your car is acceptable in the grand scheme of your relationship.

THE OREGON TALE

A simple example of a win-win solution is the situation Brad and Lisa went through. Living together for two years and unmarried, Lisa was offered a promotion that required a move from their Los Angeles home to Portland, Oregon. Brad's company couldn't provide any support to help him get established in Oregon. They both definitely wanted to stay together, but Brad wasn't sure whether he could find a comparable job in Portland. After much discussion of Brad's concerns about being out of work and Lisa's wanting to take this job to maintain her career trajectory, they decided that Lisa would loan Brad enough money to keep him going for six months—enough time to find a job. He would move to Oregon with Lisa for that six months and aggressively look for a comparable job. If he couldn't find a job, he was free to move back to Los Angeles and take back his job there, and Lisa would forgive the loan. If he did find a job in Oregon, the amount of the loan could be rolled into a like amount of ownership of the home they planned to buy there. With a little creative thinking, they were able to overcome a potentially huge obstacle to their relationship. And Brad did eventually find a different job, one he liked. They ended up staying in Oregon and buying a home together.

PITFALLS TO WATCH FOR

Insurance and bad credit are two potential problems to be handled carefully. If one of you has bad credit, creating contracts or taking actions which move property into that partner's ownership or even cosigning for that partner gives creditors the ability to attach that property to cover debts owed them. It might be better to leave assets out of creditors' reach by maintaining existing ownership. Unfortunately, moving assets out of the account of the debtor partner won't usually work as creditors can go after assets transferred within a certain period prior to default.

A partner with no insurance also poses some issues. Just as creditors can seize assets, judgments in civil cases can reach the property of the defendant. A car accident by an uninsured partner can put assets in the other's name at risk. When it comes to the different forms of ownership that nonmarried couples can utilize, the options are numerous. We'll talk more about the specifics of the major purchase most couples make—a home—in a bit. For now, here are some suggestions that the experts at the Alternatives to Marriage Project have for unmarried couples. They believe that these couples should at the very least create the following agreements:

- Durable power of attorney for health care—spouses and relatives have the legal ability to make decisions for you, but an unmarried partner does not without you filing this document that grants your partner this power of attorney.

- Durable power of attorney for financial management— again, unmarried partners have no legal power to make decisions for the other partner unless specified in this agreement.

- Will—by legal default, without a will only relatives have access to your assets.

- A living-together (or domestic partnership) agreement—this spells out the financial aspects of your relationship. These agreements usually don't cover personal aspects of your relationship (NEVER mention gender at risk of voiding the entire contract). Agreements on nonmonetary issues (who cooks or how often you can go golfing) are unlikely to be enforced by the court.

KNOWLEDGE IS POWER

For a long time people operated under the assumption that marriage was a kind of Big Brotherish nightmare. They saw it as the government intruding once again into the personal lives and choices of its citizens. Marriage was seen as a legal and social quagmire flying in the face of the best intentions of human nature at its finest. Well, those who held those beliefs are entitled to that opinion, but in my humble opinion anyone who enters into any kind of partnership without knowing what the legal ramifications of that union are, or establishing clear and legally binding boundaries and stipulations is in for an unpleasant surprise at some time. Because so many laws and statutes vary from state to state with regard to marriage and other domestic arrangements, we can't possibly cover them all. But it behooves you to know before you enter into any kind of arrangement to learn as much as you can about the nature of the agreement—whether implied or stated—in the area in which you live. Do you know if you live in a no-fault divorce state? Is your state a community property state?

Too often too many people wait until it's too late to learn what the rights and obligations of their union are. You don't want to be sitting in a courtroom or in a law office to learn what you should have known before you signed that marriage certificate or you took out that lease or bought that home with your partner. I don't want to come across as too much of an alarmist here, and I know that you intend to stay together, but the numbers tell us otherwise. Protect yourself, protect your assets, and most of all, be prepared and knowledgeable.

BUYING A HOME

For most of us, it's the American Dream. For most of us, it's the largest single outlay of cash in our lifetime. For most of us, it's the definition of success, the means by which we can say to ourselves and to others, "I've made it. I'm an adult. And this patch of God's little green acre is mine." Today, given low interest rates, a proliferation of lenders, and other market forces, purchasing a home is easier than ever. Owning a home, given those same influences, is harder than ever. Given the lower qualifying standards for loans, the increase in low or no down payment loans, the number of adjustable rate mortgages, balloons, and the like, some areas of the country are seeing foreclosures and defaults on home loans substantially increasing in the last two years. While this may be good news for real estate speculators, it points out that the dream can turn into a nightmare unless you are well-informed and well-prepared to take this step.

Marshall and David were two such well-prepared individuals. Though most people when they looked at them thought that two people couldn't be less ideally suited to one another, in fact, they have forged a rock-solid relationship of seventeen years. Marshall is nearly six feet four inches tall, a former collegiate and professional beach volleyball player, and David is a comparably diminutive five foot seven. Marshall is thirty-nine, and David sixty. Marshall now teaches junior high science and coaches. David has just recently sold his three jewelry boutiques and considers himself a man of leisure—though Marshall doubts his partner will ever be able to sit still for more than five minutes.

Marshall is a fairly typical Ritz-Carlton. Though he has never lavished himself in luxury, he has a thing for automobiles. He has never kept one for more than eighteen months to a year, and if a new BMW Z-4 convertible caught his eye, well then that's what he would buy. They depreciate so fast, he reasoned (incorrectly), that he might as well get rid of them before they lost too much of their value, so when the next shiny thing caught his eye—a Nissan 240-Z—he'd trade up. Besides, he was young, single (this was before things turned serious with David) and he didn't own a home, so he could devote more of his income to an automobile than most people. When the two of them first came to my office, it was clear from the start that David did not understand, appreciate, or want to tolerate what he referred to as Marshall's "vehicular promiscuity." If the two of them were going to merge finances, then it was time for Marshall to settle on a car so the two of them could purchase a house together.

David was a classic Econo Lodger. Though he'd taken some risks in expanding his business, in the back of his mind his parents loomed large. They too had been small business owners, only they had designs on being LARGE business owners. They owned a young women's clothing store that they eventually expanded to six regional stores. When they tried to expand beyond that to twelve in a short period of time in an ambitious move, they struggled mightily when their mall stores flopped. Their bankers called in a couple of loans and soon those liquidation sale signs were plastered across the windows of all their stores. His parents never recovered. Understandably, he was cautious, squirreling away his annual nut in case the chokers he sold suddenly turned to financial nooses.

Even when he inherited a healthy chunk of change from his previous partner upon his passing, David stayed in the neat but not extravagant townhouse the two of them shared.

Because of the unequal assets each brought to the table, Marshall and David had a lot of negotiating to do in order to choose a residence for themselves. David was particularly sensitive about the issue of using any of the money that he had received from his deceased partner Frank. He felt that he would be disloyal to his deceased lover if he spent any of it on Marshall. Consequently, when the two of them spoke about a house, there were a number of associated emotional issues they had to attend to besides the hard-and-fast bottom line numbers. On his own, David could have afforded a house somewhere in the $500,000 to $750,000 range even though he was no longer working. Marshall could have afforded something in the $250,000 range if he was willing to take one of the riskier financing options available to him. They talked about it, ran some numbers, looked at their net worth worksheets, and settled on a range of $300,000 to $350,000. They set out looking. Now, in Southern California, homes in that price range in areas they wanted to live were going to be difficult to find. Most would be characterized as fixer-uppers or small, older homes.

Among their criteria was a minimum of three bedrooms—they wanted one to be a library and the other a guest bedroom. They had to have a two-car garage, and eat-in kitchen, hardwood floors, and a fireplace. They were flexible on the last two, and in the back of David's mind was always the possibility of remodeling and expanding. Much to their surprise, it was Marshall who maintained good price discipline. The realtor the couple worked with did her best to edge further and further from the maximum price they'd told her, showing them a couple of "near your limit" homes that were clearly in better shape and in trendier neighborhoods. David fell hard for a brick and ivy three-bedroom cottage with a terra cotta tile roof, but the asking price was $425,000. As much as he wanted to offer on it, Marshall had to quash the idea. If they were going to stick to their fifty-fifty mortgage payment agreement, then that was out of his price range. He hated to disappoint David, but he had to.

Marshall's insistence paid off when, three weeks later, they found a very similar home, just three blocks outside the truly desirable zone in West Hollywood in an area undergoing gentrification. The owner was highly motivated, agreed to pay their closing costs, and accepted their offer, which was $10,000 under asking price. In his mind, David immediately spent the $10,000 on upgrades to the kitchen and all was well.

Timing Is Everything

David and Marshall's story is a good one, right? Happiness all around. Despite their income differential and their vastly different money styles, they worked it all out. Marshall and David's story isn't instructive in one way, however; they already had enough money to make a 20 percent down payment, could have covered all their closing costs, moving expenses, and the like. For many couples, the decision to buy isn't immediately followed by a purchase—they have to come up with a savings plan to get money for the down payment, closing costs, and so on.

If you've ever rented for a long period of time, you don't need to be reminded of this, but you were essentially burning your hard-earned dollars every month you wrote that rent check. No fun at all. For most of us in the real world, the one major tax write off we get to enjoy each year is our mortgage payment. We also build equity in our home, and as you can see from the table below, the value of homes has risen greatly in nearly every market in the country over the last five years. Owning a home can be a good investment, but as is true of most things in this life, timing is essential. Some say the real estate "bubble" is about to burst, but even if that is true, the damage done by that bursting will be minimal and won't affect everyone. When you compare the bubble bursting to the cost of

renting, the choice remains even clearer. If you can reasonably afford it, buy.

As you can see from the table in Figure 7-1, if you had good
timing and bought a home in any of these areas, it would have
increased in value quite a bit—in some areas more than in others,
obviously. Because we can't account for the needs, tastes, and desires, of everyone in this book, we chose the most middle-of-the-
road example to illustrate the highs and lows of property values
across the country. What's most instructive is likely to be the median—the exact center between the highest and lowest values—
which represents a gain in value of $138,240 in that five-year
period. That represents an annual gain of $27,648 in value. That's
a pretty good investment. No one can guarantee this kind of gain
will continue.

A lot of people decided to cash in on this bubble and put their
homes on the market, sold them, then used the profit to purchase
a larger, more expensive (some would say artificially high-priced)

FIGURE 7-1. Increase in housing costs.

	2000 Value	Adjusted to 2005
HIGHEST		
San Jose, Calif.	$708,600	$1,267,295
San Francisco	567,400	1,052,350
Honolulu	372,700	765,240
Washington D.C.	332,100	769,255
Los Angeles	326,300	798,140
MEDIAN	*$208,900*	*347,140*
LOWEST		
Jackson, Miss.	$126,500	161,850
Winston, N.C.	123,200	162,790
San Antonio, Tex.	122,600	166,950
Ponca City, Okla.	119,700	158,470
New Johnsonville, Tenn.	116,200	151,620
Augusta, Ga.	104,600	141,040
Tyrwanda, Pa.	101,800	164,115
Nachez, N.Mex.	93,300	137,410
Port Arthur, Tex.	82,000	105,800

STUDY: Based on a 2,200 square foot, eight-room, four-bedroom, two-and-a-half bath home in a middle-
income suburban community. Surveyed 300 metro areas.

home, and took advantage of a low rate or low down payment financing offer. I'm not here to judge, but the Data Darling in me is a little bit suspicious of this strategy long term. If some of those people had come to me, I would have suggested that instead of sinking all the profit into a new home, why not invest some of it in the market and find a similarly priced home that still suits your family's needs? Maybe college tuition wouldn't seem quite so burdensome. And are you really going to get a better night's sleep in your mini-mansion when concerns about your retirement are parading across your subconscious like a line of kick-stepping Rockettes? But that's just me.

How Much Can We Afford?

If you ask your friendly neighborhood mortgage broker, he'll tell you a very different story than what I'm about to say. I've got nothing against mortgage brokers or institutional lenders, by the way. They provide a much-needed service, but it's important to keep in mind that that "service" is also a profit-generating enterprise. The more they lend you, the higher the interest rate they can get you to pay back, the more money they make. Simple, right? As a consequence, keep this ballpark figure in mind when determining how much you can reasonably afford.

> Price Range: Five to ten times your combined annual income.

Keep in mind that your definition of "reasonably afford" and everyone else's definition of that concept is going to vary widely. Again, as you are saving for that first home or considering upgrading, live for a few months with that new mortgage cost as a part of your budget. Try it on. Take it for a spin, see how it feels.

Other Considerations

The toughest hoop most couples have to leap through is the down payment. As I mentioned earlier, probably the single highest check amount you're ever going to write is for the down payment on your home. Some scary numbers can come up when you consider how much you're going to put down. Ten percent loans are becoming more common, but the tried and true 20 percent remains the gold standard and could earn you a lower interest rate. Cash gifts from parents, grandparents, and magnanimous friends are always a possibility to help you get over that hump, but lenders expect full disclosure and can examine your financials to determine your suitability, so don't expect to be able to get away with not acknowledging how that $10,000 deposit magically showed up in your account.

If you and your partner are unmarried and you are mingling assets for a down payment, be especially careful of gifts and so on. The IRS may view the money received by one partner as a gift to the other. For tax purposes, there are limits before gift tax kicks in. Setting up the gift as a loan that is gradually forgiven might make sense for larger amounts—taking a second mortgage for instance. In addition, make sure that if ownership interests are different from the ownership interests shown in the deed that you create a contract that specifies the terms. For instance, you might contribute 100 percent of the down payment and your name is on the deed. Your partner, just getting on his or her feet financially, will contribute 50 percent of the mortgage payment and gradually earn equity in the property. Make sure you create a contract that specifies this arrangement. Otherwise, you will be assumed to own 100 percent of the property since your name is the only one on the deed.

How Do We Finance It?

I've heard a number of stories from first-time home buyers recounting the doubt and uncertainty they experienced the first time they applied for home financing. You mean someone is going to trust me with that amount of money? This is a totally irrational thought if they knew their credit ratings (if you don't, get your report as soon as possible) and what their salaries and so on would, generally speaking, qualify them for. Like a Worst-Case Scenarist, many people harbor fears that somehow the lenders will learn that they spent more than $2,000 for shoes the previous year. (Not that anyone I know would spend that much.) There are many good resources available online and in the bookstore to help you with the ins and outs of home purchasing, so we'll just give you a few basics here. Many different instruments exist to finance your purchase. Recent years have seen a proliferation of variations on these basic themes:

Fixed 30—Best if you are staying a while, rates are low, and you prefer the security of an unchanging payment.

Fixed 15—Same as Fixed 30, but paid off more quickly (higher payment) and usually a lower rate.

ARM—Great if rates are projected to fall and you don't plan to stay more than about seven years.

No Down—Makes sense for those with good earning power but little money to contribute right now. Some risk of negative equity (selling for less than you paid and thus not covering the mortgage when you sell) if home prices decline.

Forms of Ownership

How you legally own your home has a lasting and very consequential impact on your finances and legal obligations. Make sure you think about it before just filling in a standardized title form.

For an unmarried couple, buying a home together probably means that the "To wed or not to wed" discussion has occurred or will occur soon. Many emotional issues go into that decision. Buying a home has so many legal and financial implications that it is probably a good time to figure out the emotional issues because changing your situation later results in complicated tax and ownership issues. In addition, even if you don't marry it can be expensive to change ownership. If you own separately and then decide to put your partner on the deed later, you have just given a large gift and created a sizable gift-tax liability.

Getting things settled beforehand makes things much simpler.

At the real estate closing, you sign all those papers and take title to your new home. Talk with your lawyer and financial planner beforehand to ensure that how you own the property fits your situation:

- You or your partner could own the property alone. The deed/title lists only one of you as the owner. The other is merely a tenant or guest with no ownership rights. A married couple would rarely hold their home this way. With a second marriage and children as heirs, you might be tempted to keep your house in your name alone so that the home goes to your children. Through a will or a trust you can more clearly ensure that your children receive the house. Unmarried couples may choose this, especially if only one earns enough to use the tax benefits of home ownership. It may also be helpful if one partner has creditors chasing after their assets. The non-owner partner is in a risky situation, though, because the owning partner has complete control over the home. In one case, I have a client who was previously married, as was her husband, and she got the house in the divorce settlement. She continues to have sole ownership of that house, and he will have no claim to it should this second marriage go belly up.

- You could own the property together in one of two forms. Any two or more people can own property together. You don't need to be married or even a couple. You can be "tenants in common" and spell out ownership interests. As tenants in common, you share ownership of the property in any percentage you choose. If one of you dies, the other does not receive his ownership interest. It passes to the deceased owner's heirs. This could cause problems for an unmarried couple as the heirs may have other plans for the home than letting the partner stay in the house. A will or trust could specify that the surviving partner gets the other's share, but without a will the partner has no claim. If you are married, it may reduce your estate, so it makes sense for estate-tax purposes.

• If you are married, you might be more likely to own the property in joint tenancy. Joint tenancy (some states add the phrase "with right of survivorship") means that you share equal ownership of the property and have equal right to its use. If one of you dies, the other automatically receives the deceased's share of the property. As we'll learn in the estate-planning section, this is good because it avoids probate court and gives continuity to the surviving partner, but it may be bad if your estate is of sufficient size that a substantial estate-tax credit will be wasted. And a breakup would mean that you would have to legally sort out how to divide ownership.

Planning for Buyout

I know. I know. I'm doom and gloom again. But in the interest of preparation, it is a good idea to have a plan in place to help deal with an unfortunate turn of events—the dissolution of your couple-hood. Again, a simple contract that you and your partner draw up spelling out the terms of this agreement—whether you are married or not—is a good idea. It's an especially good idea if the two of you aren't married—remember that how the courts handle these issues varies state by state. How you feel about the unwritten or even un-spoken agreement the two of you have at the beginning of your relationship can be very different from how you feel once it is end-ing. If you have open and honest communication prior to the emo-tionally gut-wrenching end, then chances are you can carry over the financial bliss of your union into your independence.

8

CHILDREN AND COUPLEHOOD

D id you know:

- 40 percent of unmarried households have children.

- Births to women between ages forty and forty-four continue to rise and set records, doubling since 1981.

- Between 2002 and 2003, the birth rate for women between thirty-five and thirty-nine also rose by 6 percent.

So what's this all mean? Well, obviously people are electing to have kids later in their lives. That can be a good thing. You are more likely to be economically secure in your mid thirties to late forties. That can be a bad thing. You're incurring the expenses associated with having children later and later in your life and expenses like college tuition keep rising. Can your increased earning power continue to outpace those rising costs? This chapter will give you some ways to make sure that it does.

So, okay, this chapter didn't start out by talking about the pleasures of parenthood. Now, don't get me wrong. I love children. I really do. They bring an abundance of joy into the lives of their parents that is unquantifiable. You know that. I know that. We also know that raising children costs money, and perhaps nothing in life so fully illustrates the irrational economic behavior of us humans as having children. Those psychic rewards are most certainly worth all the money and effort we put into raising children because the numbers certainly don't add up.

Well then, does it even make sense to talk about preparedness when it comes to the question of raising children? I think so. Again, it is possible to just go with the flow and deal with the question of raising a family on a more emotional level. Are we ready for the responsibility? Are we ready to give up some of the freedom to travel, to spend, and so on that we enjoyed in our childless state? Are we even going to consider our financial picture, or are we going to dip our toe into the water and simply deem that it feels right and dive in after? Any approach will work, but we're advocating for a better balance between emotion and logic.

Just to give you a sense of what you are about to undertake financially, here are some statistics:

The cost of raising a child from birth to age seventeen

If your pre-tax income is:	You're likely to spend:
Less than $41,700	$134,370
From $41,700–$70,200	$184,320
More than $70,200	$269,000

Source: U.S. Department of Agriculture, 2004.

Note: Not included in the above estimates are the following considerations:

- The additional health and lifestyle costs of pregnancy and prenatal preparation.

- All of the hidden "new-baby" expenses.

- The cost of a break in one's career.

- College tuition. College costs have risen faster than inflation and in 2004 averaged $11,354 per year for public schools and $27,516 per year for private schools.

- Single-child households should multiply all estimates by 1.24, what I call the No-Hand-Me-Downs-Factor.

- Parents with three or more children spend 23 percent less on each child.

- Parents spend more money per year on older children than on infants.

DEFYING CATEGORIZATION

Because such a huge and widespread gap exists in our economic behavior, I don't know that any of the behavioral categories we've discussed in this book naturally fit into a discussion about having children. I can't say that Ritz-Carltons are more likely to want children or have a bigger family or that those risk-taking Texas Slims have more children. And once children enter our lives, we all use emotion a lot more than reason in dealing with the financial aspects of raising our children. Does it really make good financial sense that our four-year-old toddles around in eighty-dollar Nike sneakers that have a foot life of about three months? Probably not, but damn they look cute on him and well, when he goes to preschool what are all the other parents going to think if they see him shod in shoddy shoes? That's not a criticism, by the way, just another dose of reality. We all do it. Does that make it right? When it comes to our kids right and wrong seem to take on a different dimension.

Just think of the discussions you've had regarding allowances. When should they start getting it? Do they need to earn it or should it be given to them so that they learn how to manage it? How much should it be? What should they be able to spend it on? What should they be required to purchase for themselves? Logic and experience might dictate a certain answer, but our own childhood experiences, our emotional feelings about our parenting responsibilities, and the personalities and superb negotiating techniques of our children all play into the solution we eventually decide upon. Multiply all those feelings and discussions when thinking about issues such as education, music lessons, driving privileges, and appropriate attire.

WE ARE FAMILY

For the purposes of this book, I'm going to use the term "family" to describe any household in which two adults reside with at least one minor. We all know the various permutations and combinations that result in today's society with children from previous marriages or relationships living with children of the other partner and so on. To simplify things, we're going to talk about Mike and Carol. They each had three kids with another partner. Mike was never married, but Carol was and divorced her first partner. Both adults got full custody of their offspring, and now are living together under one roof. Defying all the odds and bowing to the gods of irony, Mike had three boys—Bobby, Peter, and Greg. Carol had three girls— Cindy, Jan, and Marcia.

Because Mike was never married to the mother of his three sons, on the advice of his Uncle Charlie a prominent divorce attorney in West Covina, he had an agreement drawn up with his partner Mary Richards to deal with the eventuality of the demise of their relationship. When Mary took a job in Minneapolis, Mike couldn't imagine uprooting his life and his boys' life in the warmth of Southern California for the frigid Upper Midwest. The split was more or less without rancor, and Mary made her monthly payments to help with the upkeep of the boys. All was rosy until Mike met and eventually married Carol. Even though Mike and Mary's agreement spelled out that she was to continue to send child support payments until each boy turned eighteen years of age regardless of Mike's relationship status, something struck her as unfair. Good thing Mike's Uncle Charlie had the foresight to draft that agreement.

For Carol, her arrangements were similar, only in the context of a negotiated divorce settlement. A Data Darling down to her very core, Carol did her homework and knew that she was more likely to keep her support payments in the wake of a remarriage if she and her new spouse agreed to keep their earnings and their ownership of property separate. Ever the accomodator, Mike was eager to please and signed off, knowing that courts in some states have held that joint income could not be considered in making a child support award when the custodial parent and new partner had such an agreement. Alimony rules, on the other hand, run the gamut. Some states terminate alimony when the recipient begins cohabiting, and cohabiting has been very broadly defined by the courts. Other states require not only cohabitation but a child with the new partner before alimony is terminated.

ADOPTION OPTIONS

If either Mike or Carol were to adopt the COGs (Children of the Opposite Gender) of the other, the formal process of adoption would eliminate support payments. Here again, parents enter an emotional minefield. How do you balance your demonstration of commitment to a child and formal separation from one natural parent with the realities of fewer financial resources to raise the child (that is, if the child was benefiting from support payments from the natural parent)? Much complex negotiation has to go on in these cases, and the pros and cons weighed. One possible advantage is that adoption makes inheritance much clearer and simpler—the adopted child would have the same rights as the biological offspring should you die without a will. What is the potential impact on your natural children, or even on children from this relationship? What if you are making support payments for children not living with you?

UNMARRIED WITH CHILDREN

No matter what the state of a couple's union, one thing is clear. The two people who created a child's life are legally responsible for their children. Courts don't care why people have children. If a child arrives, both biological parents (married or not) have a duty to support that child. That said, it is crucially important for a father to acknowledge paternity. If he's not certain that he's the father, he should register that uncertainty as well. At times, even signing the birth certificate isn't legal proof of parenthood. As coldhearted as all this may seem, and as much as I despise deadbeat dads, I can't advocate for anyone being forced to financially support a child who is not his own. On another pragmatic note, it is crucial to know who a child's parents are to establish inheritance, child support, custody, adoption, and many other rights and responsibilities—not to mention what health issues they may have.

Laws vary from state to state regarding adopting your new spouse or partner's children, but those laws and the process of adoption are usually pretty straightforward. Remember, though, that both biological parents must agree to adoption unless one has abandoned or failed to establish a parent-child relationship. If you don't adopt, you risk losing access to your partner's children if you should separate. Once again, that emotional and financial tight-rope walk begins.

PAYING FOR EDUCATION

Given the skyrocketing cost of higher education, Uncle Sam has come up with some generous programs to help us pay for college. Of course, the IRS will continue to allow Hope and Lifetime Learning credits to offset your current income tax bill; savings bonds can accrue tax-free income if applied toward college tuition; and individual retirement account withdrawals are not fully penalized if used toward college expenses. (Exceptions exist to each of these statements, so speak with a tax professional before assuming you qualify.) But the big story is the savings programs that give you benefits for prepaying your college bills—sort of a layaway program—or setting up a savings account earmarked for college bills. They are full of rules, but if followed properly they can make a large dent in your college costs.

Qualified Tuition Programs (QTPs), also named "Section 529" plans, allow you to either prepay a specified beneficiary's future education expenses or to establish a savings plan that will pay those expenses in the future. Like a Roth IRA, after-tax contributions are made into the plan but it grows in the account tax-free. When the money is taken out, it is tax-free as long as it doesn't exceed the eligible expenses. The prepayment-type plans don't have that problem since they strictly prepay directly to the school you intend your child to attend. Prepaying usually freezes costs at today's level, which could save you a bundle when you consider the potential for a huge cost escalation by the time the beneficiary reaches college age. Given how quickly college tuition rates are rising, this is an attractive option.

Another benefit of these plans is that anyone can establish one for the student—it's not limited to parents. Grandparents, aunts, uncles, godparents, or other benefactors can create such an account for the student. But be wary that the contribution is considered a gift and the tax rules regarding gifts apply. Don't worry too much if your student decides to attend a school other than the one the designated contributions have been going to, or doesn't attend school at all, you can get your money back or transfer the benefits to another child. One downfall continues to be the fact that your eligibility for other forms of financial aid may be compromised. When schools and other financial institutions calculate your eligibility for need-based grants and loans, they include the money in these accounts as available family contribution, thus reducing your need and the financial aid you're eligible for. In addition, if your distributions exceed expenses, taxes will be imposed. Also, keep in mind that you don't have the option to direct your own investments—the institution you make the prepayments to has that control. How much your dollars earn is essentially out of your hands. Some of you Data Darlings and Texas Slims, and even those Worst-Case Scenarists with control issues may not be comfortable with this notion.

There are significant differences from plan to plan on the details of how they work and are administered, so you'll need to do a lot of homework to decide on the appropriate plan. Prepay plans used to lock you in to a certain school or a certain state, but now they are joining forces and groups of schools are offering the program together so that you have more flexibility in where your child ends up going.

Coverdell education savings accounts, sometimes called Education IRAs, are another savings instrument with tax benefits. Coverdells aren't limited to use for college; they can be used for elementary and secondary school, too. You can have both a 529 plan and an education savings account for your student, although the benefits cannot exceed the eventual expenses. Distributions also must be coordinated between the two plans. Like a 529 plan, education savings accounts take after-tax income, allow it to grow tax free, and provide for tax-free distributions for qualified education expenses. Unlike the unlimited contribution to a 529 plan, education savings accounts are maxed out at $2,000 per year and fall further at higher income levels. More than one account can be set up for each individual (grandparents can also create one for the grandchildren), but the total annual contribution per *beneficiary* still can't exceed that $2,000 limit.

One advantage that education savings accounts have over pre-payment plans is that they allow you to direct the investment of the account. Those of you with control issues or risk-averse types will appreciate that benefit. Those of you who prefer to let someone else do the hard calculations and choices will likely opt for a 529 plan. Any money in the education savings account must be distributed by the time the beneficiary reaches age thirty, and you will have to pay taxes on any distributions you ultimately don't use for eligible education expenses.

YOU'VE GOT CHOICES

As you can see, a number of options are available to you to help take care of those education expenses. Deciding which one works best for you and your individual needs is a matter that you should discuss in one of your Financial State of the Union Meetings. Just like any other expense that you might incur during the course of your couplehood, planning, open communication, and prioritizing are the keys. So, obviously, is time. With a $2,000 annual cap (at best) on an education savings account, and the average cost of one year's tuition at a state school being roughly $12,000 and $28,000 at a private school, the magic of compounding interest is going to have to be your friend. A recent trend toward students taking five years instead of four to complete their education also means that you could be potentially footing an even larger bill. Go to www .collegeresults.org to see the four-year graduation rates for all colleges and universities in the United States. The top school in the survey—The Citadel (the Military College of South Carolina) graduates 60 percent of its students in four years. The national average is 29 percent. Obviously, you need to prepare for the possibility that your college tuition fund will have to be larger.

Like any other expense we've talked about, you will have to make some changes in order to compensate for the income that goes into your 529 plan or the education savings account. Since we've shown you other examples of this, I won't go into much detail here. Figuring out where that $2,000 will come from is a challenge that you and your partner can face head on. As I hope you realize by now, little changes can have a big effect when you have long time horizon and you invest so that compounding interest can work for you. The key is to get started as early as possible.

Other options do exist of course. Many states have very fine junior college and community college programs that are low cost and can help your child make crucial decisions about what area of study to concentrate on in the final two years of undergraduate work. Of course, if you know that you are a Ritz-Carlton, and you have your eyes on an Ivy League or upper-tier private education for your child, this may not be an option. You'll have to plan and budget accordingly. Also keep in mind that each year hundreds of thousands of dollars in financial aid doesn't get awarded simply because no one applies for it. Since college education is such an expense, savvy planning and investigative work is crucial. You know this expense is coming, so there is no excuse for not being prepared for it. In the next chapter, we'll continue to trumpet this message of preparedness and having a strategy in place to meet some "unexpected" life events. It's enough to make you think I graduated from The Citadel isn't it?

BEING PREPARED FOR EMERGENCIES

"Eeew, I hate when that happens."

These are the immortal words of Billy Crystal's *Saturday Night Live* New York City cop character who kept trading stories with his pal about all the self-inflicted calamities they shared. Not all of life's problems are self-inflicted or could be so easily solved.

Even the best laid plans can get derailed by something out of the blue. To get quoty one more time, life is the plan B that happens to us while we try to accomplish plan A. Things don't always go according to plan. The purpose of this book has been to help you and your partner accomplish financial bliss through this process:

Knowledge → Power → Control → Security → Bliss

138

Save and invest and you'll have the financial wherewithal to remain self-sufficient and secure. But, sometimes life proves that we don't have absolute control over our destiny. One illness, one accident, could change our situation permanently. Our only alternative is to plan ahead and develop some protection against things we can't control.

The great (in some people's estimation) writer and philosopher Friedrich Nietzsche said, "What does not destroy me makes me stronger." If you know anything else about the man's writings, then you probably understand why I'm a bit skeptical about his approach to life. While it's a good thing to bounce back from adversity, when we're in the throes of some daunting experience, there are times when it sure doesn't feel like we'll get through it, never mind benefit from it. We search for any glimmer of hope and help to impel us forward. At times like this, couplehoods can be severely challenged and the communication skills we described earlier become invaluable. There are many important decisions to be made, and very little concrete data about the future on which you can base them. How long will you be out of work? Will you ever be able to attain the same salary you had before? Do we need to drastically cut expenses, or will this be a temporary issue we can manage through our emergency fund? What if you need to relocate? Will your partner be able to go with you? How long will your parents need care? You have no real answers, just a long decision tree of "What ifs?" that flow from each other. What do you do?

One of the best ways to deal with adversity is to remain flexible. Just like your muscles need to be trained and stretched in different directions in order to be lithe and nimble, you need to prepare in advance for many contingencies. You also need to have multiple options to help deal with some of life's less pleasant moments. A plan committed to a single path with little available flexibility runs the risk of ruin. For example, if all your funds are tied up in one long-term investment, you become more of a gambler than an investor. Likewise, if you place all your bets on remaining totally healthy and productive forever and never facing any sort of problems, you are gambling with your security and the welfare of those who depend on you. Taking just a few steps can ensure that you'll be able to deal with much of the financial possibilities life can throw at you.

CLASH OF THE MONEY PERSONALITIES

At times of crisis, the differences between Data Darlings and Drama Kings become even more obvious and difficult to settle. On the one hand, a Data Darling may lend clarity to the situation and be able to see the situation through. On the other hand, a Data Darling could rationally perceive that the situation is so bleak that all hope is lost. Or they may employ logic too quickly to a situation and end up seeming cold and distant when all the Drama King wants is to be comforted or have his fears aired. Sometimes, though, hope is exactly what's needed in the face of seemingly insurmountable odds. A combination of clearheadedness and optimism bordering on hope might be just what the situation requires, so relying solely on Data Darling might not be enough. Each partner needs to bring his or her individual strengths to the table to get the relationship through whatever rocky shoals it is navigating.

For unmarried couples, the situation can be a little more complex. Without the legal bonds of marriage, your commitment to each other is reliant on whatever domestic partnership agreement you've created and your individual ethical beliefs. Granted, married partners have the "out" of divorce and unmarried couples can be ethically committed to each other more than any marriage certificate can define, but it's just human nature to look for (but not necessarily act upon) possible escape clauses when things aren't going your way. You certainly want to support and care for each other, but there is always that gray area where two people's definitions of support and care do not coincide. If you both share the issue it might be easy to decide. For instance, if your shared home burns down, even though it was in only one partner's name you both might gladly contribute to its replacement. However, if one of you faces the decision about whether to lend support to a financially struggling sibling it might not be a clear-cut decision. Talk to each other using the techniques we've discussed throughout the book. Hash out a decision and support each other.

WE'VE AGREED, BUT . . .

The domestic partnership agreement you and your partner worked out years ago may not cover whatever issues you are now facing. Or, whatever you've agreed upon might not be helpful in resolving the issue to your satisfaction. Do you renegotiate? Make an exception for this particular event? Do you hold your partner to the letter of the agreement? These are difficult issues that can only be resolved through heartfelt communications. One thing to keep in mind—in contract law, a history of exceptions to an agreement may make the exception part of the contract.

You've heard me say enough about the importance of preparation and communication by now, so I simply ask you to insert your favorite quote from your own life here. It can be about a time when you could have or should have been better prepared, a time when someone else rode to your rescue through their preparedness, or a time when you pulled one out of the figurative fire and saved the day yourself.

Okay, I can't resist. Here's something I just realized about the word "emergency." It contains the word "emerge." That's the hopeful part of all this. You will emerge from this particular set of circumstances. You can do many things in advance of and during this state of emergency to prevent it from becoming a catastrophe or a tragedy. Keep in mind that as bad as things may seem at the moment, this doesn't mean that you are at the end of your life or relationship with your partner. The word "emergency" also contains the word "merge." This means that no matter if your life together has diverged, the two of you can unite again and get through this. So, okay, I may be wandering into Cheesyland here, but cheese has a long shelf life and makes an excellent emergency ration when stored properly.

Now let's get down to the specifics.

CREATE A RAINY DAY ACCOUNT

One of the most important steps you can take to prevent an emergency from becoming a catastrophe is creating a fund to cover living expenses in case of an interruption in your income or some catastrophic loss. The interruption could be the loss of a job, a disability, a sabbatical to care for an ill parent or child, or moving to another location before each of you has a job. Accidents, crime, and lawsuits could overwhelm all your financial efforts and plans. Before you even begin investing, the emergency fund should be established. I don't want you to stuff the money in a mattress or coffee can in the basement, and you don't need to open a secret Swiss bank account. You do need to use an investment that is extremely liquid and extremely safe. Treasury bills, short-term government bonds, money market mutual funds that hold Treasury bills or bonds, bank savings accounts, or certificates of deposit, and their equivalents make a good place to invest without undue risk. Sure, you're not going to earn earth-shattering returns, but the point is safety and piece of mind. Once this base of safety is established you can become a little more risk tolerant in the rest of your portfolio.

How much should you put away? Some advisers think a six-month cushion is sufficient. Yes, disability insurance helps in some cases, but in many instances it takes some time before the cash actually reaches you. Circumstances dictate how much you should actually save. If you rely on your paycheck as your sole source of income, you should have more of a cushion. Likewise, if you are a one-paycheck couple you should maximize the emergency fund. On the other hand, if you have a good-sized passive income source or if you are in a position in which the loss of one paycheck won't be immediately devastating you could stay on the lower end of the funding scale. Another factor is the liquidity of your current investments. If you have stocks and bonds that you could easily sell, you might be able to reduce your emergency cushion. I'm not suggesting dipping into your individual retirement accounts and such, but an existing portfolio of liquid assets itself would provide some cushion. It's still important to have a distinct emergency fund, because you don't want to be caught dipping into long-term savings too much or at a time when you might have losses or inordinate tax consequences. To be conservative, only view last year's profits on your stock and bond portfolio as part of your emergency fund.

INSURANCE

Insurance should be a cornerstone of your rainy day protection. I don't make a blanket recommendation that everyone needs every conceivable form of insurance at all times. Depending on your stage of life and financial health, insurance in its various forms can be helpful in getting you through some of the events that put a burden on your finances, but it could also be an expensive proposition. A study by the Insurance Research Council, reports that couples spend about 16 percent of their annual incomes on insurance, but fewer than half aggressively shop for coverage; the majority defer to agents who may have vested interests in selling one type of policy over another, and many people buy policies from the first company they contact. Remember the old joke about the guy who goes into a doctor's office and raises his arm over his head and says, "Doc, it hurts when I go like this." Without looking up the doctor says, "Don't go like that."

Well, the same is true for shopping for insurance and buying from the first company you contact. Here's where having a Data Darling on your team will really help. You'll need insurance against one of them injuring you if you don't do due diligence on your insurance research. It will hurt a lot more in your pocketbook if you don't do research.

How Does Insurance Work?

The concept behind insurance is to get lots of people to put small amounts of money into a big pot and offer to make them whole if some low probability but high expense event should occur. Insurance companies manage the pot of money and make the payouts to the hopefully small group of people who have claims. They keep policy expenses low by investing well and managing the level of risk they take. Too many payouts or too little investment income lead to higher insurance premiums. And, of course the insurance company takes its profits out of the pot, too. Depending on your financial personality and your own experiences, you can view this as a sleep-at-night necessity, a necessary but no-win situation that subsides others' losses, or a that's-the-way-it-goes cost of living. I believe it serves a useful purpose if bought intelligently, and here are several types of insurance that every couple should investigate if not hold.

Life Insurance

Life insurance is important when others rely on you for their financial support. There are two basic reasons to buy life insurance. One is to provide dependents with financial support if you should happen to make a premature exit. With the insurance proceeds, they'll be able to carry on without your financial support. The other is to provide funding for your final expenses so your passing will not place a financial burden on your loved ones. Both of these are admirable goals and worthy of some funding by you. The life insurance industry has developed products that are quasi-investments and life insurance can play a role in your estate planning, but for our purposes we are viewing it as a risk management product to protect our dependents in case of our death.

Consequently, I advise buying the cheapest product available—term life. It is strictly an insurance policy. It doesn't accrue the investment income or cash value like whole or universal life. I think those policies are expensive for what they accomplish and not necessary for an emergency fund. When you have kids and you're just starting out, life insurance is essential and your needs are high. You have a lot of lifetime left in which your dependents are relying on you. As you move into later phases of parenthood and empty nesting, your insurance needs should decline. You have less dependency time left, and though college costs are near the end of that dependency, you might be in better financial condition by that time. You'll likely be in your prime earning years and moving from a net borrower to a saver.

By the time you retire, life insurance may not be a good deal. Prices go up with age, and the financial devastation of your demise should fall. However, if you are in a position that you are reliant on any cash flow that will be reduced if you die, life insurance might still be a good idea at retirement. For instance, if your spouse's life expectancy exceeds yours and your joint and survivor pension will decrease subsequent to your death, it may make sense to have life insurance on you if he or she wouldn't be able to survive on the proceeds of your estate and the reduced pension benefits. If you read this book and follow its advice you shouldn't end up so reliant on a single income source; nevertheless, review your pension and other retirement plans to determine whether this is a possibility. That said, it's always best to buy life insurance when you are young—that's when whole life can be your cheapest buy.

The nice thing about term life is that you can stay flexible and change it as you review your needs. You can get it in various terms of five, ten, and twenty years or for longer. You can cancel and move to another company or another amount. It is readily available at good prices on Web sites as well as through traditional brokers. On the downside, later in life you might need to pass a physical for some companies in order to be insured. Just one more motivation to eat right and exercise. Keep in mind that it will have no cash value for you.

Unmarried and Insured

Being unmarried isn't really a complication when it comes time to purchase life insurance. You can purchase a policy on just about anyone and name nearly anyone as your beneficiary—your partner, your children, your first-grade teacher. Just make sure that you keep your beneficiaries up to date if your situation changes. You own the policy and can change it at any time.

Disability Insurance

The same arguments for and against life insurance apply to disability insurance. When you are young and with dependents it is important that they have some protection in the event that you are not able to work. If the bulk of your income is derived from investments and not work, your income would not be in jeopardy if you were to become disabled. As you move into empty nesting, your own expenses must still be covered even if you have no nonworking family members depending on your income.

To calculate how much disability insurance you need, first figure your monthly take-home pay after taxes. Next, call Social Security to find out how much Social Security would pay if you were disabled. (Many cases of disability do not qualify for Social Security benefits, so you should probably not count on receiving any.) Next, ask your company benefits manager what kind of benefits you would receive if you were to become disabled. Now, add up any other sources of income you may have, such as investment earnings, and subtract the total from your current monthly take-home pay. That's how much you need in disability benefits to maintain your current after-tax income.

If you decide you need a disability insurance policy to supplement the benefits you already have, look for the following:

When do benefits begin? Most insurance companies give you a choice about how long you have to wait before benefits begin, anywhere from thirty days to a year. The longer you are willing to wait, the lower the premium. Check to see what resources would be available to you immediately following a disability and choose the longest waiting period you can reasonably handle.

How long should benefits last? It's probably wise to have benefits continue until you reach age sixty-five when Social Security starts.

How is disability defined? This is a tricky one because disability can be defined in many different ways. Does it mean you can't do any work at all? Does it mean you can't do your regular work? "Own occupation" policies are more expensive, so you may have to plan on switching careers if you encounter a disability that prevents you from performing your regular job. But that may not be so bad. The main thing you're insuring against is loss of income.

There are specific rules regarding taxation of disability payments. I spoke with Alin Wall, a CPA, RBZ, LLP, who offered this summary:

Generally speaking money received under a disability insurance contract for loss of earnings arising from illness or accident is tax exempt. In addition, the premiums are not deductible. However, if the disability insurance premiums are employer paid, the disability benefits become taxable. If you want to keep the benefits tax exempt, your employer must include the premiums in your W-2 income or you must fund the premiums yourself through reimbursement to the employer.

Again, when in doubt, contact a professional adviser about the best course of action.

Unmarried Couples   Because the benefits are paid to you, the disabled person owning the policy, there should be no problems whether married or unmarried.

Health Insurance

If you've encountered any recent medical problems or suffered an accident recently requiring a long (or even a short) hospital stay, you've experience what we all know. There is a health care crisis in this country. Health care costs are certainly out of control, and that makes it even more vital that you have coverage. Accidents, the high cost of treatment for a mounting list of ailments, the possible loss of income if you don't have disability insurance all means you just can't afford to get sick or injured. But how much control do you have over that?

According to a report posted on the Web site of Health Affairs (www.healthaffairs.org) citing 2001 statistics, nearly 1.5 million American families filed for bankruptcy. Based on those filers interviewed, the people at Health Affairs estimated that as many as 2.5 million people (those who filed and their family members) were affected by what is now termed "medical bankruptcy." In other words, they were filing as a result of some medical costs they incurred. What is most disturbing is that the vast majority of those who filed for bankruptcy and cited medical costs as a contributor had health insurance coverage. If our health insurance can't keep us from bankruptcy, what kind of insurance is that? We've been hearing for years about health insurance reform in this country, yet little real progress seems to be being made, and the crisis is deepening. As is true throughout this book, I'm not encouraging an alarmist "the sky is falling" mentality. We all need to be aware of the possibilities that exist and be as prepared as possible for the new reality.

Most people rely on their employer-sponsored health plan for checkups and the occasional trip to the doctor for various minor ailments. They assume that if something really major were to happen, like cancer or heart disease, the health plan would take care of it. Don't be so sure. Most health plans have lifetime limits. If you need more care than the plan will play for, your own assets will be at risk. You may not have much choice about which health plan to use, but you should always check the lifetime limits of the plan and consider purchasing an additional major medical policy to cover really horrible illnesses.

Also, be sure to fill in any insurance gaps that may occur when you're changing jobs. The federal law known as COBRA (short for the Consolidated Omnibus Budget Reconciliation Act of 1985) allows you to continue with your employer's health plan for eighteen months after you terminate; however, you have to pay all the premiums out of your own pocket. This means health insurance that cost you, say $50 per month when your employer was subsidizing most of the premium, could now cost you $400 or $500 per month. Some people take the risk, letting their old health plan lapse on the assumption that they will quickly find another job that offers a good health plan. This can be dangerous. If your job search takes longer than you expect or you're diagnosed with a serious illness, you could find yourself uninsurable.

There's a provision in the federal HIPAA law (Health Insurance

Portability and Accountability Act) that says you may not be denied insurance, even if you have a preexisting condition such as diabetes, as long as you have had continuous health care coverage. If you do have a gap in coverage, it may be no longer than sixty-three days. Individual states can increase the period if desired. So, if you forego COBRA and wind up with a three-month gap in your coverage, you would lose your HIPAA protection when you later decide to buy insurance. You would then have to wait the full preexisting condition period imposed by your new carrier's policy.

Unmarried Couples   Slowly, some local governments and some employers are offering domestic partner benefits. For the most part, though, you are each on your own for health benefits. You could talk to your human resources benefits representative to find out if your employer will agree to cover your partner on its health plan if you pay for the premiums. Employers' group plans are usually less expensive and provide better coverage than the plans available to individuals.

Generally, married couples can be held liable for paying the health care costs for the other, over and above what is reimbursed by insurance. Unmarried couples, on the other hand, remain free of liability for the health-care costs of the other. Only half of the assets held jointly and all of those held in the liable partner's name can be attached by medical collectors.

Again, be absolutely sure that you have a durable power of attorney for health care (or health care proxy) and one for financial management naming your partner to make decisions for you if you are incapacitated. Without them, your partner has no legal ability to make important decisions on your behalf if you should become incapacitated.

Auto Insurance

Automobile insurance is another type of insurance you cannot afford to go without. Some states mandate minimum coverage in order to protect the other party in an accident, but to protect yourself it might be better to opt for more. You can get the most for your money by being smart about your driving habits and policy selection. The thing that has the most dramatic impact on the cost of insurance is the value of your car. Drive an old clunker and you'll pay next to nothing in insurance. (Be sure to cancel the collision and comprehensive; they're not worth it on an old car.) Other ways to reduce your car insurance premiums are to raise your deductible and cancel any medical coverage that may be duplicated in your health insurance.

Unmarried Couples   If you have separate vehicles and keep your driving separate, you should have no problem finding separate insurance. If you want combined insurance, either because you jointly own your vehicles or because you share driving of each vehicle, it may take some shopping around to find an insurer. Not all companies offer such policies, and fewer still offer the discounts and other special benefits married couples would receive.

Homeowners Insurance

You wouldn't think of going without homeowners insurance—and neither would your lender. It protects you against both the loss of your home and belongings in a catastrophe and from the result of a property-based legal judgment against you. Even though the odds of your house burning down or a major robbery occurring are, thankfully, very slim, the consequences of such disasters, if they were to occur, could devastate you financially. In the case of homeowners insurance, you are happy to pay into the big pot and hope never to take anything out. That's why you'll want to review your policy every so often to make sure it still meets your needs.

How much coverage do you need? Experts recommend that you base your insurance on replacement value rather than market value or the amount you paid for the house and its contents. After all, if disaster strikes you will need to rebuild and replace, so these other methods of valuation are meaningless. Insurance companies have guidelines based on square footage, building material, and other criteria, but you may want to do your own estimates after talking with contractors and factoring in any special features you may want in a replacement home, such as fancy moldings or custom hardwood floors. Remember that replacement value may have nothing to do with market value. Market value includes the house and the land. Replacement value is just the house, and even some of the house, such as the foundation, may not need to be replaced. Even so, the cost of building a new home could be substantially more than buying an existing home. Homeowners policies used to include a provision guaranteeing "full replacement value" even if the replacement cost exceeded the amount of insurance carried. Recently, however, insurance companies have determined that this is not economically feasible and have shifted the onus of keeping property coverage up to date back to the policyholder.

Ideally, you should insure your home for 100 percent of its replacement value, but in any case no less than 80 percent. Insurance companies require that you carry at least 80 percent of replacement value in order to be fully reimbursed in the case of a partial loss. If you carry 80 percent and sustain a $10,000 loss, you will receive the entire $10,000; but if you carry only 60 percent, (three-quarters of the required 80 percent), you'll receive only $7,500, or three-quarters of the damage. Don't make the mistake of insuring up to the value of your mortgage. That would protect the mortgage holder but cause you to lose your entire equity in the home.

What about inflation? If your homeowners policy does not have inflation protection and you haven't changed your policy in several years, this would be an excellent time to revisit your policy. In most areas of the country, the building boom resulting from low interest rates has resulted in higher building materials costs. Even at low levels of inflation, the cost of building a home can escalate before you know it. On the other hand, if your policy does have automatic inflation adjustment, check to see that it hasn't boosted your coverage and your premium higher than necessary.

What about that diamond brooch? If you've collected a lifetime of personal treasures like jewelry, antiques, artwork, and furniture, you probably need extra coverage for these items. Most homeowners policies cover only $1,000 or $2,000 for things like jewelry, stamp collections, and silverware. So take an inventory of what you have, get an independent appraisal of the more valuable items, and sit down with your insurance agent to see what you have to do to make sure these items are covered, whether it's adding a rider to your existing policy or taking out an additional policy. One again, we'd like to suggest that you use your judgment when buying any kind of insurance. Sentimental value can never be replaced no matter how much insurance you carry.

What about liability? If a deliveryman slips on your sidewalk and breaks his leg, your homeowners policy should cover the costs associated with a lawsuit. Still, there may be certain limitations, so check with your insurance agent to see if you are adequately covered for mishaps that happen to other people while in your home.

What about floods and earthquakes? Floods and earthquakes are horrible disasters that don't happen very often, but when they do, they leave their victims in total financial ruin. That's why most homeowners policies don't cover them. If you want protection against floods and earthquakes, you must take out separate policies, which can be expensive. You can mitigate the cost somewhat by having a high deductible. Or you can go without and hope for the best. As we've seen recently in south Florida and the Gulf Coast region, these natural disasters take a terrible toll on the living as well as on the victims who've lost their lives. I know of one particularly telling story that breaks my heart. A woman I know recently built a new home in New Orleans. The contractors finally finished in June of 2005 after she spent millions on it. Well, as you know, Katrina came knocking down doors, houses, and lives, in August of 2005. Her home was inundated by flood waters and is a total loss—contents and all. She was wise enough to pay for flood insurance, but according to her carrier, she wasn't insured for this disaster—what caused the damage was the faulty levees. That's a man-made object, and no act of God or natural disaster.

To make matters worse, she was also engaged to be married to a man who made significantly less money that she did. Now that she's been wiped out by this disaster, their relationship has taken a 180-degree role reversal. She finds herself living with him, being supported financially by him, and I'm very curious to see how this all plays out.

Unmarried Couples   Homeowners insurance is readily available and comparably priced for unmarried co-owners. Trouble arises if one of you isn't an owner of the home. Only the owner's property is covered by the policy, so the other partner should purchase a separate renters' policy to cover his belongings if their value warrants coverage. If you are renting rather than owning, joint renters' policies are easy to get whether married or not.

Credit Insurance

Credit insurance takes many forms. It can be a policy that will pay your mortgage off if you should die. It can be a policy that makes your monthly credit card payment if you should lose your job or become disabled. The concept sounds good, and that's what the marketers of these products bank on. Don't buy them. These are high-priced policies that you don't need if you have life insurance or the other insurance products I recommend. Insurance companies are in business to make money by pooling a little money (relatively speaking) from a lot of people to cover a risk that is small in probability but great in impact. They assume that if you are willing to buy such credit insurance you are probably in a higher-risk category, and they charge accordingly.

OVERINSURED VERSUS UNDERINSURED VERSUS MISINSURED

Okay, so here's the million-dollar question that's likely to be running through your head. I know from reading this section that Americans average about 16 percent of their income on various forms of insurance. Great. But does that mean that's the ideal amount I should spend? Of course not. Does that mean that all Americans have adequate insurance to meet all their needs? Of course not. Should I ask my insurance company or my agent if I am overinsured or underinsured? You can. Should I trust that I'm getting the right answer? Of course not. Disclaimer: I have nothing against insurance agents. I have several very fine ones. But the job of an insurance agent is to *sell* you insurance. That's how she makes her money. Unless you have a wonderfully close relationship with all your insurance providers it is too much to expect that they all will answer you with 100 percent honesty. Better yet, do some independent investigation. A quick scan of Amazon.com produced thousands of results for books on insurance, including the usual Dummies and Idiots guides and the like. A Google search of the term "over insured" turned up more than 31 million entries. Personal finance magazines are another good source of information about how much insurance you need based on your individual needs.

Your best bet is to consult with a certified public accountant. An expert can cut through much of the interference and speed the process of evaluating your insurance needs. Whatever investment you make in securing their services will be earned back in savings and peace of mind that you have an advocate working for you.

YOUR MONEY STYLE AND INSURANCE

Depending upon where you and your partner fall on the risk scale, you may look at insurance as a necessary evil, a necessity, a fuzzy warm security blanket, or something to be avoided entirely. You and your partner need to understand one another's position relative to risk in this area as well as investing. Risk is all about the issue of control, and all of the various emergencies and contingencies we've discussed could raise your eyebrows or the hair on the back of your neck. Be sensitive to how your partner responds not only to your discussion of these issues directly but to stories about other people and their insurance, health issues, and trials and tribulations. You can infer a lot about their attitudes and values from those responses. Those cues can help you as you negotiate with your partner on insurance issues and emergency contingency plans. Obviously, if one of you has had a family member, particularly a parent, fall victim to something like medical bankruptcy, then that partner may be more vigilant about insurance issues. Sometimes vigilance can come across as paranoia, so you need to be careful about how you express your fears.

For example, when Marshall and David took a look at their combined financials, they bumped up against some interesting issues that they had to discuss and eventually work out. Marshall knew about David's previous relationship and how he came to inherit a substantial sum—a portion of which came from his deceased partner's life insurance policy. In addition, another complicating factor was their age difference. Chances were that David would die before the thirty-something Marshall. To make matters even murkier, Marshall didn't want to appear as though he was interested in getting his hands on any of David's money—he initially advocated that David not purchase any additional coverage. When the two men first tentatively tiptoed around the issue of life insurance and beneficiaries, they were trying so hard not to step on one another's toes that it was truly a case of two steps forward and two steps back. David had been through an emotionally draining experience and his survivor guilt and an unease born of insecurity about why a young man like Marshall was with him reared its hair-thinning head.

Like most couples neither of them could come right out immediately and reveal all of the feelings they were harboring, but in time, after a series of talks over a few weeks, they managed to come to an agreement. Insurance, in general, cut against the grain of Marshall's devil may care attitude (except when it came to insuring his cars) and set against David's risk-averse nature, much give and take had to go on. Eventually, David took out an additional life insurance policy with Marshall as the beneficiary. The amount was just enough to cover David's portion of the mortgage—he wanted to be certain that the house the two of them bought together would stay with one of them for as long as possible.

David's situation was unique as well because of his recent retirement, and it is to this next life event that we will turn in the next chapter.

RETIREMENT

At Long Last and
How Long Will Our Money Last?

I f there's one thing that most adults look forward to, it's any break from the routine of work—a lunch break, an out-of-office meeting, a vacation, and ultimately, when we finally stop being ordered around by our alarm clock, calendar, or BlackBerry forever. Hopefully, all the discipline required to remain gainfully employed for the vast majority of your adult life will have rubbed off in other areas of your life. I hope that as you approach retirement, you'll do so with the same sense of anticipation that you did when you were counting down the days to a vacation.

Think about a few of those vacations, though. Some of them you'll fondly recall as among the most enjoyable moments of your life, and some of them you'll recall as events you'd rather not recall. Chances are whether you look at a specific vacation as the former or the latter, the reason why is because of the amount of planning that went into the trip. Those plans don't just include where you chose to go and what you did once you got there, but, we hope, how you were going to budget for it and pay for all the fun. I don't know if I could imagine anything worse than having to spend the entire time you were supposed to be having fun worrying about your funds.

Well, I wasn't perfectly honest with you. I can easily imagine something worse than that—worrying about your funds during your entire retirement. After all, would you rather think of your retirement as one long uninterrupted vacation or as an extended period of anxiety? After all, there are going to be other issues besides finances that are going to take some getting used to in retirement. Few of us realize the dramatic emotional impact retirement has on us and on those around us. This might be the most critical time for a couple to plan together and talk to and support each other.

For many of us, in retirement we may face an identity crisis, a shift in how we define ourselves and how others view us. We lose the structure and comfort of work—even if we sometimes looked at our career as a kind of prison term. The reality settles in that we are nearing the end of our lives. With freedom comes the need to figure out new ways to define success. Our relationships shift. After years of effort, we may have just settled into a comfortable routine with our partner. With retirement, we may be utterly baffled trying to figure out how to redefine our roles and figure out who this person we've spent so many years with has become.

WORK ETHIC AND EFFORT

Work still defines most Americans' lives. It is how you create your worth and provide productive activity to benefit society. Some of us are defined by our work; some even become workaholics. We think of our foremost role in life as our occupation. Whether you enjoy your job or not, it absorbs your life and adds structure to it. You feel useful. It takes up your time, occupies your thoughts, puts food on your table, and provides social outlets. From nine to five, you know where you will be and what your duties are. When all of that vanishes, you can easily become lost. You are left to your own devices to find a role that has meaning to you. Do you spend all of your time enjoying leisure activities? Do you keep your house cleaner than ever? Do you watch the grandkids? Volunteer? Find another job mentoring younger workers? So many options, but which ones will actually satisfy you and leave you feeling useful? It's almost like going through the late teens all over again and trying to figure out where you fit in the bigger picture.

We all know of someone who was so wrapped up in their work that retirement was like prison to them, and many of them die soon after retirement. People who have tied nearly all their identity to their work and have little else in their lives have the hardest time with retirement and need the most support from partners and others close to them. Don't ask me how I know. I am one of them. I constantly talk with my husband and friends about this issue. What am I going to do? I need a hobby! Talking and planning are vital. Flexibility allows for more room to experiment and figure out what role will work for you.

LIFE'S INEVITABILITIES

Thoughts of our death and our legacy also become more prevalent after retirement. Sure, life spans are increasing, but we are still on the down slope of the bell curve. If we've accomplished all our goals we can feel satisfied but also restless for new goals. Regrets for what we haven't accomplished can gnaw at us, but hopefully might move us toward finding a different way to succeed and leave our mark. Volunteering has helped many older adults find happiness and fulfillment while helping others. Starting another career might be a way to leave your mark. Be inspired by Colonel Harlan Saunders, who didn't create Kentucky Fried Chicken until after retiring and realizing he didn't want to live on his Social Security check.

Besides our individual issues brought on by retirement, couples have their own issues. I can't tell you how many of my just-retired clients tell me they wish their partner would just stop getting in the way in the kitchen or garage or would just get out of the house for a while and do something because they're disrupting the other's long-established routine. Couples who have been together for a long time have (unconsciously) developed well-oiled routines. Things run pretty smoothly and they each understand their roles and habits. When retirement rolls around, each searches for things to do or a break from the normal routine. As a result, tension and chaos can take over until things get sorted out again. This is a silly and simple example of the way couples must reevaluate their positions within their couplehood. You might not realize all that your partner does, especially for the relationship. You might not know how to contribute more effort around the house. Just getting used to being together more is an issue. Privacy may be compromised. Time for personal hobbies and interests may have to be renegotiated when one partner wants more time together. Couple-directed activities take over. It becomes almost like dating again as you rediscover each other.

STARTING OVER

Married couples may have informal, unspoken contracts with each other, and unmarried couples may have wisely established formal contracts about how to manage certain aspects of their relationships. With retirement, many of those contracts won't work anymore. With all of the changes that take place and all of the opportunities that become available, couples must put a lot of effort into talking about their new reality: from changing incomes to figuring out whether to move and downsize; from who should do the cooking to whether one of you wants to go back to school or start a new career; and how much support you should provide your parents and children.

Certainly, use the communication tools from chapter 3 and try to plan as much as you can before retirement arrives. But, know that you can't plan for every contingency and you won't know how it feels until you get there. So, remain flexible and continue to look for ways to feel fulfilled and support your partner's fulfillment.

For all these reasons, your Financial State of the Union Meetings (you have been having them regularly on the lead up to retirement haven't you?) should take on a new purpose and may perhaps develop a new sense of urgency. Just as you did when you first started this process toward financial bliss, it's important to do some assessing, selecting, and goal setting.

ADDING IT ALL UP

Earlier on, I defined financial bliss as security. In so many ways, having your finances in order and having sufficient money buys you security. For some of us, the motivation is freedom. We fought the good fight. We put effort into careers, family, and all the other things that are important to us. We're looking forward to the freedom that comes from reducing our "responsibilities" and figuring out our passions. So, let's do a little bit of number crunching. And find out how much passion you can afford.

So what if your net worth is $10 million or $10,000? The big question you really wonder about is whether or not you'll have enough money to live the way you want through your full retirement before you run out of money. I'll show you some numbers that will give you a rough estimate of the answer to this question.

Step 1: What Will the Assets You Already Own Be Worth When You Retire?

You've already done the information gathering and calculations for your present net worth. But what does that number in today's dollars translate into down the line? In this first step, you will get a clearer picture of what your financial picture may look like at retirement.

A. Which Assets Are Available for Retirement Living Expenses?   When you retire, you will still need a place to live and all the accoutrements that go along with living. You might downsize your home, sell one of your cars, and have a garage sale, but mostly you'll be relying on your liquid and financial assets to live. You might sell your collection of presidential campaign buttons or Beanie Babies, but you might also hold onto them as something to pass down to your children, wanting to sell them only as a last resort. So go back to your net worth worksheet and as a conservative estimate use liquid assets and savings and investments less any assets you cannot sell (for example, business interests, trusts out of your control, collectibles) as your funds to retire on.

B. What Will They Be Worth by the Time You Retire?   Let's see how these calculations work by following along with Bob and Lisa. Both now fifty, they've a done a good job of saving for retirement. They are in the 28 percent tax bracket right now, and will probably only fall into the 25 percent tax bracket when they retire. An abbreviated version of their net worth available for retirement as of today is:

Cash, CDs, savings accounts	$	25,000
Bond portfolio		50,000

Stock portfolio	75,000
IRA	100,000
401(k)	500,000
Other real estate	450,000
TOTAL VALUE	$1,200,000

Now that Bob and Lisa know the present value of these assets, they need to project into the future. They each want to figure out at what age they can reasonably retire and still maintain their present lifestyle. In order to do that, they have to figure out how much their assets are going to appreciate in the next few years. This is a good thing, of course, since we much prefer to see our wealth grow instead of decline. To determine how much their wealth will increase over time, they consulted the table in Figure 10-1, which shows the various possible rates of appreciation.

As you can see, these are some pretty big numbers, aren't they? If you start early and get a good return, the magic of compounding interest works very hard for you. It becomes a snowball rolling down a long hill that gets bigger and bigger as it goes and gains more and more momentum.

But the real question here is what rate should you use? The rate should be calculated by starting with the asset's rate of return and reducing it by the amount it will be taxed, to see what will finally end up in your pocket. The table in Figure 10-2 will help you do this. You also have to calculate how it will be affected by inflation, in order to put the number in terms of today's dollar.

What rate of return should you use? This is a bit tricky, since we are trying, in a sense, to predict the future. You want to use a rate that best represents the future performance of the asset. As always, past returns are no guarantee of future performance. As a general estimate, however, past performance gives some indication of the *long-term* returns. Many other factors regarding timing, individual stock picks, and diversification enter into determining how you will do. Ibbotson Associates is the bible for returns on various assets and stock market sectors. Their stock market and bond data is strong all the way back to 1926. According to their research, average annual returns have been as shown in Figure 10-1.

FIGURE 10-1. Worth of an asset at retirement that is worth $100,000 today.

Years To Retirement	Average Annual Appreciation Rate						
	2%	4%	6%	8%	10%	15%	20%
5	$110,408	$121,665	$133,823	$ 146,933	$ 161,051	$ 201,136	$ 248,832
10	121,899	148,024	179,085	215,892	259,374	404,556	619,174
15	134,587	180,094	239,656	317,217	417,725	813,706	1,540,702
20	148,595	219,112	320,714	466,096	672,750	1,636,654	3,833,760
25	164,061	266,584	429,187	684,848	1,083,471	3,291,895	9,539,622
30	181,136	324,340	574,349	1,006,266	1,744,940	6,621,177	23,737,631
35	199,989	394,609	768,609	1,478,534	2,810,244	13,317,552	59,066,823

FIGURE 10-2.   Income tax rates for 2006.

Rate	Income	
	Single	**Married filing jointly**
10%	Up to $7,300	Up to $14,600
15%	$7,301 to $29,700	$14,601 to $59,400
25%	$29,701 to $59,975	$59,401 to $119,950
28%	$59,976 to $91,400	$119,951 to $182,800
33%	$91,401 to $163,225	$182,801 to $326,450
35%	Above $163,225	Above $326,450
	Long-Term Capital Gains	
5%	Income up to $29,700	Income up to $59,400
15%	Income above $29,700	Income above $59,400

Type of Asset	Annual Return
Long-term government bonds	5.47%
T-bills	3.71%
Long-term corporate bonds	5.92%
Stocks overall	10.36%
Small cap stocks	12.64%
Real estate[1] (NAREIT Index)	9.75%

[1]Since 1985 only.

Bob and Lisa will use these percentages to calculate how much their assets have appreciated.

A Bite out of the Future   Unfortunately, inflation reduces the value of your savings and needs to be factored into your calculations. If you are now retiring, you likely started working somewhere around 1960. If you started planning for your retirement back then, you might have thought that you'd need $10,000 per year to live on when you retire, based on the cost of living at that time. Fast forward to 2006. If you go to the Department of Labor's Consumer Price Index Web site and plug in the year "1960" and the amount "$10,000," you would be shocked to find out that the $10,000 you figured in 1960 would actually need to be $67,128.40 in 2006 in order to have the same buying power! In the forty-five years of your working life, prices have gone nearly seven times higher, an annual increase of 4.3 percent! In other words, the dollar you saved in 1960 is only worth about 15 cents today. Even the mild inflation of the past twenty-six years (3.44 percent per year since 1980) has eroded a 1980 dollar down to 41 cents.

By subtracting inflation upfront in your calculations, you'll have a better ability to estimate the amount of money you'll need in the future. You can use today's prices to estimate what your future cost of living will be. So, if monthly living expenses are $1,200 now, you don't need to review every item and decide what it might cost when you retire, for instance. Use today's amounts and estimate an over-all inflation rate over the period you're examining.

Figure 10-3 shows the calculations for Bob and Lisa. To make things simpler, we'll assume their individual retirement account is in bonds and the 401(k) is in stocks. Many factors affect the actual tax rate on individual retirement accounts and 401(k) withdrawals, but for our purposes here we'll just assume that they'll be taxed at the long-term capital gains rate.

We used the long-term capital gains rate for everything but the cash. Bob and Lisa won't be withdrawing money until they retire, so they'll benefit from the lower capital gains tax rates. With cash, the income will be earned throughout the savings period, so it is ordinary income.

Round off the actual net gain result (5.4 percent for their stock portfolio) and go to Figure 10-1 to see what it will grow to. For their stock portfolio, look in the 6 percent column and 15 year row to find the result "$239,656." Multiply today's amount ($575,000) by 2.39656 ($239,656 divided by the $100,000 from Figure 10-1 you started with) to get your result. Add across the "Available Amount" columns and you'll see that Bob and Lisa end up doing well even after inflation and taxes—nearly $2,400,000.

If they want to retire earlier, the calculations are essentially the same: Instead of using the fifteen-year column, they would use the five-year column so they could see the difference made by those additional ten years of earning returns on their investments.

FIGURE 10-3. **Estimated worth of Bob and Lisa's assets in fifteen years.**

Bob and Lisa's Current Holdings

Cash, CDs, savings accounts	$ 25,000
Bond portfolio	50,000
Stock portfolio	75,000
IRA	100,000
401(k)	500,000
Other real estate	450,000
Total Value	**$1,200,000**

	Stock Portfolio	Bond Portfolio	Investment Real Estate	Cash (use T-Bill rate)
Today's Amount	$575,000	$150,000	$450,000	$25,000
Asset rate of return:	10.36%	5.92%	9.75%	3.71%
Multiplied by: (1-tax rate)	85%	85%	85%	72%
Result	8.8%	5.03%	8.29%	2.67%
Subtract the inflation rate	3.4%	3.4%	3.4%	3.4%
Actual net gain in today's dollars	5.4%	1.63%	4.89%	−0.73%
Multiplier from Figure 10-1—15 years at actual net gain rate	2.39656	1.34587	1.80094	0
Available Amount (in today's dollar value)	$1,378,022	$201,880	$810,423	Less than $25,000

Step 2: How Much More Can I Accumulate?

The numbers we calculated for Bob and Lisa in the previous section showed how much the assets they now own will be worth when they retire. But they should be able to continue saving for the next fifteen years until retirement. What will that be worth?

Again, the snowball into an avalanche miracle of compounding interest can help you. If you start early, the effect is huge. If you start later, you'll still get some benefits. You'll just have less room for error should long-run returns temporarily disappear. Looking at your present net worth and any windfalls that might come your way before retirement, you can use Figure 10-4 to discuss how much of your current income you want to put away for retirement.

Again, to use this table properly, adjust the return by taxes and inflation.

Bob and Lisa feel that they can save $20,000 per year over the next fifteen years. They're going to invest in a blend of assets and feel that they can earn a 6 percent rate of return. In Figure 10-4, a $10,000 annual cash flow for fifteen years is worth $232,760 in today's dollars, so $20,000 annual cash flow is worth twice that, or $465,520.

Step 3: Add It All Up

The previous two items represent the amount of money you'll have available to you for living expenses during your retirement. For Bob and Lisa, the total they'll have to live on if things go as they plan are:

Value of Current Investments	$2,400,000
Value of Anticipated Savings	$ 465,520
Total Available for Retirement Expenses	**$2,865,520**

Sounds like a lot of money, doesn't it. But, how long will it last? That depends on two things—how much you spend each year and how long you live.

HOW MUCH WILL YOU NEED TO SPEND EACH YEAR?

For many people, living expenses really don't decrease during retirement. Sure, if you're now in the throes of paying for college or raising several children, your expenses may fall. But the expenses

FIGURE 10-4. If you save $10,000 per year, when you retire you will have . . .

Years to Retirement	Average Annual Appreciation Rate					
	2%	4%	6%	8%	10%	15%
5	$ 52,040	$ 54,163	$ 56,371	$ 58,666	$ 61,051	$ 67,424
10	109,497	120,061	131,808	144,866	159,374	203,037
15	172,934	200,236	232,760	271,521	317,725	475,804
20	242,974	297,781	367,856	457,620	572,750	1,024,436
25	320,303	416,459	548,645	731,059	983,471	2,127,930
30	405,681	560,849	790,582	1,132,832	1,644,940	4,347,451
35	499,945	736,522	1,114,348	1,723,168	2,710,244	8,811,702

specific to you as a couple and the maintenance of your household really stay pretty constant. Will your mortgage be paid off by then? Will you travel more or less? Will you take up golf or some other hobby? Will you be spoiling your grandchildren? A lot of questions to sift through to come up with a realistic answer.

Never ignore the impact of taxes when you plan your retirement strategy. In the first two steps of the process, we adjusted for taxes and inflation, so you don't need to do so again in figuring your retirement budget needs. However, don't take that to mean that taxes are inconsequential and that tax planning is not an issue. Taxes do matter, both in the actions you take to get to retirement and in how you spend your money during retirement. It all gets very complicated and caveats abound, but in the end Uncle Sam seems to have given us some breaks no matter what our situation. For instance, in general, the money invested in individual retirement accounts goes in pretax and comes out taxable. Money invested in Roth individual retirement accounts goes in after tax and comes out free of tax. Other accounts are taxed depending on what you contributed versus what represents gains or how you to decide to eventually take the money out.

And don't assume that your tax bite will go down after you retire. Depending on how well you saved, your income may not decline that much. And deductions may go down if you pay off your mortgage, move to a smaller home or less expensive area, and reduce some of the dependent and employment-related deductions that you relied on in the past.

We've also ignored Social Security and private pension payments for now, but you can net them out of the amounts you'll spend annually. Social Security now sends all of us a periodic statement telling us what our accumulated benefits are and what our monthly payment will be. If you believe that Social Security will remain unchanged until you retire, you can include those payments in your calculations. Too, many private pension funds are underfunded and their ability to meet their obligations by the time the horde of Baby Boomers retire is still a question mark.

How Long Can You Live on Your Accumulated Assets?

Some experts have looked at long-run returns, the outlook for the stock market and the cost of living, and increasing life spans and have pronounced that spending 4 percent to 5 percent of your nest egg each year of your retirement is the correct number. (See Figure 10-5.) Individual circumstances, especially health and your local cost of living, certainly affect that result.

FIGURE 10-5. What percent of your retirement savings can you spend each year to last your remaining lifetime?

Percentage of Your Retirement Savings Spent Each Year	Average Annual Appreciation Rate During Retirement								
	−4%	−2%	0%	2%	3%	4%	5%	6%	10%
2%	26	34	50	Forever ....
3%	20	25	33	55	Forever ....
5%	14	16	20	25	30	41	Forever ....
6%	12	13	16	20	23	28	36	Forever ....
8%	9	11	12	14	15	17	20	23	Forever
10%	8	9	10	11	12	13	14	15	20
15%	5	6	6	7	7	7	8	8	9
20%	4	4	5	5	5	5	5	6	6
25%	3	3	4	4	4	4	4	4	5

Bob and Lisa are going to reduce their ongoing expenses somewhat, but their desire to travel and enjoy life a little more will probably soak up any day-to-day living expense savings they might accomplish. To be conservative, they're assuming that their expenses will not decrease from the $85,000 per year that they currently calculate. Going back to their tally of their available retirement fund, $85,000 per year represents about 3 percent of their accumulated wealth. If they put all their money in bonds, which have earned 4 percent per year after adjusting for taxes, their money shouldn't run out, no matter how long they live.

The picture looked so rosy, in fact, that they decided to consider retiring early. You can see how the numbers work out in Figure 10-6.

The result, about $1,880,000, was nearly $1 million less than if

FIGURE 10-6. **An estimate of what Bob and Lisa's assets will be worth if they retire in ten years.**

Cash, CDs, savings accounts	$ 25,000
Bond portfolio	50,000
Stock portfolio	75,000
IRA	100,000
401(k)	500,000
Other real estate	450,000
Total Value	**$1,200,000**

	Stock Portfolio	Bond Portfolio	Investment Real Estate	Cash (use T-Bill rate)
Today's Amount	$575,000	$150,000	$450,000	$25,000
Asset rate of return:	10.36%	5.92%	9.75%	3.71%
Multiplied by: (1-tax rate)	85%	85%	85%	72%
Result	8.8%	5.03%	8.29%	2.67%
Subtract the inflation rate	3.4%	3.4%	3.4%	3.4%
Actual net gain in today's dollars	5.4%	1.63%	4.89%	−0.73%
Multiplier from Figure 10-1—10 years at actual net gain rate	1.79085	1.21899	1.48024	0
Available Amount (in today's dollar value)	$1,029,739	$182,849	$666,108	Less than $25,000

they saved and let it grow for another five years. If they added in the $131,808 that their $20,000 per year additional savings would be worth over ten years you get to about $2,060,000. Was it still something they could live on? The same $85,000 per year that they thought they would spend worked out to about 4 percent of their nest egg. Again referring back to the table in Figure 10-5 and assuming the same 4 percent rate of return, they would still have enough to live on no matter how long they lived.

Lisa, being the risk-averse partner, wanted to know whether things would work out if they should not be able to earn as much as they thought. What if they earned 2 percent less on each asset class?

Doing the same calculations, they found that their retirement nest egg would be $1.51 million from their existing savings and $240,000 from additional savings, for a total of about $1.8 million. Annual spending of $85,000 amounted to 5 percent of their savings. If they continue to earn 2 percent less than they originally thought, namely 2 percent per year, they could look toward twenty-five years of worry-free retirement. If they retire at sixty, that would put them at eighty-five years of age. Lisa, with a longer life expectancy, didn't feel quite as comfortable about this as Bob did. She did the calculations again, assuming that they could cut expenses a little more during retirement—maybe down to $75,000. That worked out to 4 percent of their savings per year, putting the life expectancy of their savings at about halfway between the twenty-five and fifty-five on the chart—so about forty years. That would get both of them to the century mark, and seemed to soothe Lisa.

Bob, being the Ritz-Carlton of the pair, wanted to see whether they could spend a little more and still have enough money to satisfy Lisa's need for a cushion. He pictured two trips a year to exotic locales, not just sight-seeing but actively pursuing many of the outdoor activities he enjoyed. He even thought Lisa would be thrilled by the romance of living in the "City of Lights" for a year, finding a *pied à terre* along the Seine in the bohemian Montmartre district and immersing themselves in the language and cooking that she loved so much. She would never do it herself, but he thought it would be such a wonderful gift for all the sacrifice she had made over the years. Back to the tables and their original assumptions, they found out that increasing their spending to $140,000, or 5 percent of their total savings, would still leave them with forty-one years of savings, again getting them to one hundred years of age. Even if their earnings rate during retirement dipped to 3 percent, they would be safe until ninety-five years of age.

Retirement planning is something that you and your partner will want to consider as early as possible in your financial life together. There are many complicated issues to consider, and even the most determined of Data Darlings may be confounded by the many choices and options, pros and cons of various strategies. As is true of many of the issues we've discussed, it's sometimes a good idea to get an expert involved. That's true even if you and your partner aren't encountering any kind of conflict in determining how you want to handle retirement planning. As I've mentioned before, consensus isn't always a good thing. Groupthink can creep in, and sometimes having a third party involved in the process to point out alternatives that the two of you might not have considered otherwise is about the wisest move you can make.

ESTATE PLANNING

t's never too early to plan for how your estate will be handled when you die. However, most of us wait and wait before we face up to the need for such planning for the final disposition of our assets. The reasons are many. When we're young, we don't think we'll ever die. When we're older we don't want to think about that looming possibility. And when we think about the legacy we want to leave behind it is usually in terms of the impact we'll have on the world rather than the worldly things we leave behind. We might think we don't have enough assets. We might think it's too complicated. By following the advice contained in this book, I hope we can take care of the sufficient assets part of the equation. The remainder of this chapter we'll try to deconstruct the issues involved so that you have a general understanding on which to base a useful discussion with an estate-planning professional.

THREE TRUTHS

The reason for estate planning boils down to what I like to call the three truths about dying. First, you can't take it with you. Second, if you don't decide where you want it to go beforehand, the state will decide for you. (And they don't do a very good job of it.) Third, if your estate's value exceeds $2,000,000—the estate exemption amount for 2006—your heirs (except your spouse) will have to pay substantial taxes on the amount they receive. A huge industry and a whole lot of complicated, convoluted legal vehicles have arisen for the sole purpose of helping you get as much of your estate as you can out of the taxman's hands and into the hands of your heirs. Do you need to know all the minutiae of all these trusts and other maneuvers? Not necessarily. It depends upon the size of your estate. Exceed the exemption and the taxman taketh. And the larger the excess, the higher the rate at which he grabs.

ADDITIONAL UNCERTAINTY

One complicating factor in planning your estate is the fact that Congress is looking at revamping the estate tax system. The exemption will increase and tax rates will gradually decline through 2009. In 2010, there will be no estate tax at all—just for that year. Lawmakers are still trying to decide what to do after that. As one way to help out the Baby Boom retirees who are financially ill-prepared for retirement, they are considering a permanent repeal of estate taxes, among other possibilities. But, as the law stands today, in 2011 and beyond, the exclusion would revert back to $2,000,000 and the top tax rate would return to 55 percent.

A SIMPLE PLAN

The basic steps in planning your estate are:

1. Figure out who you want to have your assets—the beneficiaries.

2. Figure out what assets you have or will likely have.

3. Lastly, figure out the strategies to get those assets into the right hands and minimize the amount that the Internal Revenue Service gets.

You and your partner likely can accomplish the first two and even get a ballpark number for the third before you talk to a planner. It won't necessarily be easy because a lot of emotional issues need to be addressed. Even determining who the beneficiaries should be is wrought with conflict. If you are on your second or third marriage or coupling, and so is your partner, and maybe even your children, the whole idea of who gets what might become an overwhelming dilemma. You might be tempted to forget the whole thing and let them fight it out later. Don't. This is an awful burden that can tear a family apart. You might also grapple with whether each of the heirs is able to make good financial decisions, or whether you should somehow protect them from themselves. You'll have to decide whether each heir gets the same amount of inheritance, or whether the amounts will be based on need or love or the support they provided you. Do you disinherit someone? Do you skip a generation? What's more important to you—providing for your current partner, your children, or the needs of your privately held business? Unmarried partners must also grapple with the issues of whether and how to conceptually combine their estates in order to care for their separate beneficiaries.

The second best advice I can give to those going through the initial planning stage is to talk about it with the people involved. Involve your partner in your thoughts on the subject. Feel out your prospective beneficiaries to determine whether your ideas about their needs and wants match up with your wishes. You might think you are bestowing a priceless reward on your son by leaving him your cherished 1960s muscle car. Unfortunately, you might not have noticed that the car meant little to him but he always had fond memories of watching you work in your woodshop and he would really prefer your woodworking set and some of the items you created. Such an awkward situation can be avoided by asking some simple questions beforehand. My example may sound trivial, but expand it a bit and think of the concerns if a family business that not all siblings participated in was the issue.

I don't mean to imply that you should comply with everyone's wishes. After all, they are your assets and your wishes are paramount. Yet, it would be a shame to inadvertently cause confusion, hurt feelings, or even a family rift because of some unknown or misunderstood issues. You won't be able to explain your reasoning or take a mulligan from beyond the grave.

The best advice I can give you is to speak with an estate-planning attorney. Estate planning is their specialty and all they do. As a result, chances are they've seen it all before and they will definitely know all the crucial questions to ask. In addition, they'll help you talk with your children.

For more information about the emotional and financial issues involved in this, I recommend Dr. Steven J. Hendlin's book, *Overcoming the Inheritance Taboo* (Penguin/Plume, 2004). As the title indicates, many people have a difficult time talking about issues of inheritance. The book offers some sound financial advice as well as effective guidelines for dealing with the spectrum of issues that may emerge as you work through this process.

WHO GETS . . .

If you die without any estate instructions, state law governs how your property is distributed. Generally, the laws of succession follow accepted patterns of familial relationships—spouse first, children next, parents after that, and so on. (See Figure 11-1.) But the laws vary from state to state with regard to percentages—in some states

FIGURE 11-1. **Who will get your estate if you leave no will?**

Rules vary from state to state, but most follow this general pattern of intestate (without a will) succession if you die without a will and are unmarried:

- If you have "legitimate" children from any partner, all of them receive equal shares of your estate. If any of your children die before you, their children share equally in the share their parents would have received. Daughters-in-law and sons-in-law are not considered heirs.
- If you leave no children or grandchildren, all of your property goes to your parents if they are alive.
- If you have no living parents, your siblings receive equal shares of your estate. Again, if they are deceased, their children get equal portions of their parent's share.
- If none of the above exists, your nieces and nephews get your estate. Children get equal portions of their deceased parent's share.
- If none of the above, your paternal and maternal grandparents get equal shares. And if they have died, their children get equal portions of their shares and so on until some distant relative is found.
- Lastly, if none of these relatives exist, your property goes to the state.

spouses get everything, in others the spouse and children share one-third/two-thirds, for example. And nonrelatives are never included in the estate distribution. So, the safest thing to do is to state your wishes in a will or other legal device.

You can leave your property to anyone you wish through some of the legal devices I'll describe in later parts of this chapter. At this point, we're merely concerned with coming up with the list of those who will share in your estate and what you might leave them. Partners and children usually come to mind first. But, also think about those for whom you would leave even a small portion of your estate. You can leave money to a favorite charity or a teacher from grade school who really inspired you to make the most of your artistic talents. Maybe there are other kindnesses you'd like to repay or debts, monetary or otherwise, you'd like to satisfy.

If you are married, most state laws provide default distributions to your spouse. Again, what the law provides and what you wish to do could be very different. Sit down and really determine what you and your spouse desire and require. Your spouse may be able to live on just a portion of your remaining estate and wish to downsize if you should die. She doesn't want the burden of managing the business ventures and stock portfolio that you have. To her, maintaining your car collection would be a curse more than a benefit. Maybe she would prefer that your children get some financial support because they are at a time in their lives when they could most benefit.

AFTER YOU . . .

If you think you will be the first to die, it's really not a good idea to merely leave everything to your spouse and then let her figure out what to do with everything in her will. That's not estate planning. That's passing the buck. Think through both steps. What happens when the first of you dies and then what both of your wishes are for the distribution of your estate when both of you are gone. Tragically, September 11th, taught us all how random our fates can be. That's why it's essential to consider all these issues, no matter how unpleasant or immaterial they may seem at the time, as early as possible.

Of course, situations change and any estate plan should be flexible and reviewed periodically for required changes. Maybe additional grandchildren have arrived, you have a new favorite charity due to an illness, or you decide to change your distribution levels because one of your children has become disabled and needs more help. You are certainly allowed to change your will or other instruments until the moment you breathe your last breath. An estate law expert can also help you craft estate documents that have some flexibility built into them.

If you are unmarried, it is even more vital to have estate-governing methods in place. State law does not include an unmarried partner as a default beneficiary of the estate. If you want to leave something to your partner, you will have to specify those instructions. Likewise, an out-of-wedlock child does not automatically receive the same inheritance rights as a legitimate child if a parent should die without a will. You don't have to sign a paternity statement or raise a child to leave him or her property. But to be absolutely sure your child is provided for after your death, you should have a paternity statement and affirmatively leave him or her property in your will or by use of a trust.

EXECUTOR

I love those scenes in movies when the executor, the person responsible for disseminating the information contained in a will, gathers the family, friends, and associates together for the big announcement. High drama ensues. It doesn't have to be that way, and in fact, as Dr. Hendlin advises, the reading of the will shouldn't be a time for any surprises. Let people know in advance what you intend and have in store for them. Most people aren't likely to be that forward thinking, so for our purposes, in addition to beneficiaries, you need to choose someone to see your estate through the process and ensure that your wishes are best carried out. The executor will file the will in probate court, notify beneficiaries, settle claims/debts, and see that the assets end up where you specify.

Anyone can be the executor, and you should choose someone you trust. Partners, adult children, best friends, or close relatives can be executors. Some people choose an unbiased professional, such as an estate lawyer, bank trust officer, accountant, or financial planning professional. Keep this in mind, and this comes from someone with considerable experience as an executor: You may feel like you're bestowing an "honor" on someone by naming him your executor, but it is really a lot of work, a lot of time, and a lot of responsibility. Choose wisely. Here are some suggestions:

- Don't choose someone your own age. You want someone who is likely to outlive you and be capable of handling the duties.

- Only choose a professional you know well and who is very clear about your wishes.

- Beneficiaries may not be good executors if you have any complicated financial issues or family issues. We all hope we'll be unbiased in such cases, but human nature is to give the benefit of the doubt to our own self-interest.

- Name more than one executor. Choose an alternate or a coexecutor.

WHAT THEY GET . . .
HOW ESTATES ARE CALCULATED

Your next step is to determine what you have, or will have, to leave to your beneficiaries. Hopefully, you've been following my advice and annually updating your records with additions and deletions to your net worth statement and your documents file. These form the basis for determining your estate for tax purposes, which we'll get to in a minute. But you also should go through the personal belongings that might not be worth a lot of money but are priceless in their sentimental value to you or your beneficiaries. Photo albums, treasured knickknacks that evoke fond memories, an old Army uniform, and countless other items all of us accumulate over a lifetime hold value beyond money. I know of one woman who more than anything wanted her mother's robe because it still held the scent of her mother and her favorite lotion. Another person wanted her dad's beat up old typewriter because of the memories it evoked of the letters she received from him while away at school. Think about all of these items and talk to your prospective beneficiaries to get an idea about other items they value.

Fortunately, when it comes to estate taxes, sentimental value isn't included in the Internal Revenue Service's calculation of your estate. Unfortunately, the IRS has no big, sentimental heart that gives you a break. Witness the 46 percent of your estate it will take if you die in 2006. To determine your estate tax burden, you should start by calculating your gross estate—everything you own minus everything you owe. Assets that you don't own at the time of your death are not part of your estate, so they are not taxable. The more you get rid of before you die the less taxes your estate will have to pay. Of course, you need to balance the giving away of your property before your death with the need to maintain enough to support yourself throughout your remaining years.

Ownership of the property is an important consideration in determining your taxable estate. If it is solely in your name it is part of the estate. If you hold something jointly, only your portion of the asset is considered part of your estate. For instance, if you and your spouse or partner share ownership of your home, only your ownership portion is part of your estate. If you've kept ownership of property you both use in your partner's name, it is not part of your estate. Likewise, spouses can have separate assets for estate tax purposes.

HIDDEN ASSETS

Be aware of some hidden assets that need to be included. Life insurance proceeds are only includable if you've made your estate the beneficiary, which is often not a good idea. Retirement benefits that are paid upon your death are generally included in your estate. Exceptions do exist, but usually benefits from pension plans, profit-sharing plans, and individual retirement accounts, and annuities may be taxable if proceeds remain after your death. Trusts in which you maintain some semblance of ownership or control might also be includable as part of your estate.

The final consideration in determining your taxable estate is that taxes will be paid on the value of the assets at the time you die. So, you'll need to find out the market value for each asset. For stocks and bonds, market value is relatively easy to determine. For other assets; such as business interests, real estate, jewelry, and collectibles; an appraisal is necessary. Here again, is where your documents' box and a safe-deposit box will come in handy. It's essential to let your children know where these documents are, and that they be on the account title in the case of safe-deposit boxes so they will have easy access to the information when you are gone.

Once you have the current market value, you subtract out the tax basis of each property. In theory, the tax basis represents the amount of money that you've already been taxed and that you've put into the assets. In practice, tax basis can be as simple as what you paid for the asset, or it may be extremely complicated to figure out if it was inherited or additional costs were incurred during your ownership of it.

Don't forget your debts. Just as in the net worth calculations, debts reduce your estate. If you have a $1 million home but you also have a $900,000 mortgage on it, you really only possess $100,000 of that home. Even unsecured debt like that which is on charge cards reduces your estate because lenders can legally be satisfied through the sale of your assets at the time of your death. Death does not hold off the tax collector or the debt collector. Thankfully, your heirs are not responsible for your debts, but your estate is.

From this gross estate number you've calculated, you can subtract charitable bequests and certain expenses related to managing the estate-settlement process to arrive at your taxable estate. You also subtract all property left to a surviving spouse who is a U.S. citizen. Refer to the estate tax schedule in Figure 11-2 to determine the amount of tax due on the remaining net amount, and then subtract the unified credit to arrive at your net estate taxes.

As an example, let's assume your estate is worth $995,000 when you die in 2008. This amount falls below $1,000,000 in the tax table, so we use the next lower category ($750,000) to figure the tax. Your

FIGURE 11-2.   **Estate tax rates through 2009.**

If taxable amount is more than:	But not over:	The tax is:	Plus:	Of the amount over:
$0	$10,000	$0	18%	$0
10,000	20,000	1,800	20%	10,000
20,000	40,000	3,800	22%	20,000
40,000	60,000	8,200	24%	40,000
60,000	80,000	13,000	26%	60,000
80,000	100,000	18,200	28%	80,000
100,000	150,000	23,800	30%	100,000
150,000	250,000	38,800	32%	150,000
250,000	500,000	70,800	34%	250,000
500,000	750,000	155,800	37%	500,000
750,000	1,000,000	248,300	39%	750,000
1,000,000	1,250,000	345,800	41%	1,000,000
1,250,000	1,500,000	448,300	43%	1,250,000
1,500,000		555,800	45%	1,500,000

Unified Credit Against Estate Taxes

Individual dying in . . .	Receives a unified credit of . . .	Which eliminates the tax for estates valued up to:
2006 through 2008	$780,800	$2,000,000
2009	$1,455,800	$3,500,000

tax would be $248,300 on the first $750,000 of value plus $58,500 (39 percent of $150,000) on the amount by which $900,000 exceeds the $750,000 category floor. From the tax you can then subtract the unified credit of $780,800 to find that you don't owe any taxes. Working backward from the unified credit, you can see that your estate would need to be valued at over $2,000,000 before any taxes would need to be paid. (Please note that this schedule applies to federal estate taxes only; state and local taxes are separate.)

APPEARANCES CAN BE DECEIVING

From the above description, you might think that leaving everything to your spouse is the perfect way to eliminate estate taxes.

Unfortunately, all it does is postpone the inevitable, and at higher estate levels, actually increase the taxes your combined estates will ultimately pay. The unified credit protects $2 million of estate value. With a married couple, their combined unified credits could shield $4 million of estate value. If the first spouse to die leaves everything to the surviving spouse, the deceased spouse's unified credit is wasted. The estate is not reduced—it merely passes to the surviving spouse. When the surviving spouse dies, she only has use of her own unified credit, which only shelters $2 million of the estate from taxes. If the estate exceeds $2 million, taxes will need to be paid. Had her spouse bequeathed a part of his original estate to others in order to use up his unified exemption or to get the remaining estate at or below $2 million, they could have gotten the full $4 million estate tax protection. For example, if your estate amounts to $4,500,000 when you die, you could pass it completely to your spouse and pay no taxes. Assume she dies before 2009 and that the estate remains at $4,500,000. Her estate would end up with a $1,905,800 tax bill. Had you originally left $2,000,000 to others and only $2,500,000 to your spouse, the $2,000,000 would have been protected by your unified credit—no tax. When your spouse died, the remaining $2,500,000 would have had a tax bill of $1,005,800 reduced by her estate's $780,800 unified credit down to $225,000. Your heirs would have received $1,680,800 more than if you had merely left everything to your spouse.

WHAT IS PROBATE?

Probate is a court procedure that makes sure your assets go where you want them to go after you're gone. The process begins when your executor or attorney files your will with the local probate court. If you have no executor named, or if you die intestate (without a will), the court will appoint an administrator who will handle your estate for a fee. During probate, the court will determine whether the will is valid—not forged and its provisions are legal. The court will then oversee the distribution of assets and final settlement of the estate. While there is no legal requirement that you use an estate attorney, most people do to speed up the process and to ensure that they comply with the law. Attorney fees vary and come out of the estate proceeds. Other probate costs, including filing fees, accounting fees, appraisal fees, and any other costs that may be required to protect and distribute the assets, also come out of the estate. In some cases, all those costs can eat up 5 percent or more of the estate. In addition, some states, such as California, New York, and Florida, are notorious for being expensive and time-consuming while other states have greatly reduced the probate burden. In addition, probate involves filing an inventory of the deceased's assets and liabilities as well as the actual will, and these filings are open for public inspection. In fact, several Web sites list the actual wills of famous celebrities such as Babe Ruth, Elvis Presley, and Jacqueline Kennedy Onassis. No wonder people try to avoid probate if at all possible.

HOW PROPERTY PASSES TO HEIRS

You can pass property to your heirs through:

- Gift

- Contract

- Operation of law

- Will

- Trust instrument

- Your state's laws of succession

By Gift

You can give your property away during your lifetime and enjoy the glow of helping someone. You'll also make sure that the person you wish to get it actually gets it. Those assets stay out of probate because probate is not triggered until after death. You don't necessarily escape taxes, though. The Internal Revenue Service wouldn't allow such a loophole to exist. Instead, large gifts are added to your taxable estate to determine your "gift and estate tax" bill, from which the unified credit is subtracted. In other words, the "unified" descriptor applied to the tax credit is used because it is a tax credit to be applied to the combination of large lifetime gifts and your eventual estate. At this time, you and your spouse can each give up to $11,000 to an individual in one year without incurring any gift tax. Any gift exceeding $11,000 becomes a large gift, and is subject to gift tax. However, you don't have to pay a gift tax unless the cumulative total of all large gifts you have ever made exceeds $1,000,000 (the maximum amount of the unified tax equivalent you can use toward gifts). Once you exceed that $1,000,000 amount (your spouse gets an equivalent amount, remember), you will start paying gift taxes. Also remember that any unified tax credit you use up on gifts during your lifetime reduces dollar for dollar the credit you can apply toward your estate.

When giving away appreciated property, keep in mind that the person you give it to will inherit your cost basis as well. This means he or she will eventually have to pay income taxes on it when they sell. On the other hand, if you pass it to people through inheritance, their cost basis is the value of the asset at your death. For example, let's say that you have 1,000 shares of a $10.00 market value stock that you bought for $1.00. If you give it to your daughter during your lifetime, eventually she will have to pay taxes on the $9.00 appreciation in value. If you give it to her through your estate, her cost basis becomes $10.00 and she will only have to pay taxes on the appreciation above that level. Of course, the tax man must have his due, so your estate will pay taxes on it. If you are over the unified credit your estate will be paying at a 45 percent rate. Capital gains taxes for your daughter currently don't exceed 15 percent, so if you are going to be over the unified credit a gift saves you 30 percent (45 percent estate tax rate minus the 15 percent capital gains rate) of the asset's value. Plus, it's deferred until she actually sells it.

In order to be a true gift, you must relinquish all rights to it. You can't give away shares of stock but continue to receive the dividends or remain custodian of the account. If you do, you are judged to still own it.

By Contract

Individual retirement accounts, pension plans, annuities, and life insurance are all contracts requiring you to specify one or more beneficiaries who will receive the property at your death. These contracts operate independent of the probate process and the instructions in your will, so periodically check their beneficiary designations to ensure that they still reflect your current wishes for your estate. If your individual retirement account still lists your ex-spouse as the primary beneficiary, she will get it even if in your will you stipulate that your current spouse is to get everything.

If an unmarried couple has a written agreement about ownership of their property, most states will recognize it. If the contract doesn't contradict any aspect of your will, the probate court will enforce it. Also, if any property is jointly owned; for instance, a home that both partners sign for, the deceased partner has no legal right to bequeath more than his share of the property to someone else. The surviving partner will retain the same level of ownership—or more if bequeathed part or all of the deceased partner's share.

By Operation of Law

As we learned in the "Buying a Home" section, when you hold property in joint tenancy with another person, your share automatically goes to the other person when you die. This happens no matter what you stipulate in your will. If you live in a community property state (California, for example), additional rules may apply. Property held in joint tenancy passes outside the probate process. Don't confuse the in- or out-of-probate issue with taxable or not taxable issues. Whether or not something goes through probate has nothing to do with whether it is subject to estate taxes. It only means that probate court is unnecessary for that asset because ownership is already recognized through contract.

Clear transfer and elimination of the probate process are reasons that many people prefer joint tenancy for their home and brokerage accounts. Beware, however, that if you add a joint tenant to an existing solely owned asset you are immediately giving that joint tenant a taxable gift of half the value of that asset.

By Will

A will is a written legal document that allows you to specify who should get what when you die. You may also leave instructions for guardianship of your minor children. Any adult who is "of sound mind" may draft a valid will. Although it's possible to draft a handwritten will, it's better to have an attorney draft your will to make sure it stands up in court. You can change or revoke your will at any time. You're not tied to one original will forever. In the will, you should also name an executor for your estate.

Even if you've used other methods to provide for the inheritance of specific property, it is also a good idea to include a residuary clause in your will. This clause states that any property in your estate for which you haven't otherwise left instructions will go to the named person or persons. You may have overlooked some assets or there may be some assets that really weren't meaningful enough to warrant a formal document, so you can lump them all together and in your will leave them to someone. More than likely, your partner is the logical person to receive these items, which are probably the miscellaneous items we use from day to day.

By Trust

Trusts are possibly the most useful but most misunderstood personal financial planning tools. A trust is merely a device through which you can transfer property to another person. It is a legal arrangement under which another person or institution holds legal title to property for the benefit of a third person or persons—your beneficiary. The trust document includes terms and conditions you stipulate and the rights and responsibilities of all parties involved. While that doesn't sound too complicated, many variations of trust exist to fit estate transfer issues, so we'll cover those in a separate section.

By the Laws of Succession in Your State

Remember Figure 11-1 that described how the state will distribute your assets if you are unmarried and leave no will? Unless that is exactly how you would want your legacy to be distributed, you should use any combination of these other methods to ensure that the right people get the right assets. Unless you leave instruction and cover all your worldly possessions, the state will carve up your estate as prescribed by law.

POPULAR ESTATE-PLANNING STRATEGIES

If you want to avoid probate, if your estate is large enough that you will be facing tax consequences, or if you want to put some controls on the distribution of your assets after you die you will likely enter the world of trusts. It's sometimes confusing, and giving up control of your assets is scary. You wonder how laws allow some of these valid activities to exist. There are some shady characters and a lot of wild claims are made. Once in a while someone steps over the line and new laws have to be enacted to prevent the abuse. Despite all that, some trust strategies are very effective, legally proven, and time-tested methods for managing you estate. If you use well-established and respected providers of trust services you should be safe from both shenanigans and the taxman. I'll describe some of the useful, well-established trusts in this section.

Our first step in the estate-planning process was to decide what you wanted to accomplish with your estate and who you wanted to share in your estate. Keep that foremost in your mind as you search for estate-planning advice. Don't fall for the latest flavor of the month or a one-size-fits-all boilerplate trust. Know what you want to accomplish and find someone who listens and tries to accommodate that. Don't just try to minimize taxes or whatever sales pitch the advisor lives by. If it is very important to you to leave something to someone in a certain way, then do so even if it doesn't reduce your tax bill down to the absolute minimum.

Credit-Shelter Trust for Married Couples with Over $2,000,000 in Assets

I mentioned earlier that passing everything to the surviving spouse isn't such a good idea for large estates. The unified credit of the first spouse to die goes unused, so the overall tax bill on the assets by the time the surviving spouse passes away is more than it needs to be. The credit shelter trust is set up to fully use both spouses' unified credits—hence the name. It is set up so that when the first spouse dies, the amount that qualifies for the estate-tax credit— $2,000,000 through 2009—goes into a trust instead of going directly to the surviving spouse. The trust owns the assets, but the surviving spouse receives income from the trust. So, if you have your dividend-paying stocks in the trust, your spouse will receive the quarterly dividend checks. When the surviving spouse dies, the assets in the trust go to the children (unless you specify otherwise). The assets in the credit-shelter trust are not taxed when finally distributed from the trust. The income your spouse receives from the trust during her lifetime is taxed.

Other benefits of the trust:

- The assets are professionally managed by the trustee—someone you appoint or someone the trust administrator supplies. Your spouse does not need to worry about managing the asset.

- The trust can name the eventual receivers of the assets when your spouse dies.

- The assets do not become part of your spouse's estate, so they avoid taxation as part of her estate.

- The appreciation on the assets held in trust isn't subject to estate taxes. The eventual receivers of the assets will pay taxes when and if they sell, but their capital gains tax rate is almost always lower than the estate tax rate.

In order for assets to pass to a credit-shelter trust, they must be held in each spouse's individual name (not jointly). You don't need to give up ownership of the assets the moment you sign the trust documents. You can use a so-called pour-over will, which directs the assets into the trust at the time you die.

Living Trust to Avoid Probate

Still queasy from reading about the time and cost of probate? Didn't appreciate the fact that everyone can read Marilyn Monroe's will on courttv.com? A living trust is a good way to avoid all of that.

It allows you to do the same basic job as a will while avoiding the probate process. However, unlike other trust vehicles, *a living trust does not affect your estate tax situation.* Don't believe anyone who tells you otherwise.

The basics of a living trust are simple:

- While still alive, you place any or all of your assets in the trust. Don't worry. While you are alive you maintain complete control over the assets. Law and the Internal Revenue Service still view them as belonging to you, and you have the ability to remove them or change the assets in the trust at any time since you name yourself as the trustee and put in a clause stating that the trust is revocable.

- You name a successor trustee—the person who will manage the trust when you die.

- You name the trust beneficiaries—the people who will receive the assets in trust after you die.

Pretty straightforward. When you die, your successor trustee takes the property and transfers it to your beneficiaries without requiring probate or other court proceedings.

If you also want to avoid some taxes, you can set up the living trust as an irrevocable trust. As long as the trust is revocable, the Internal Revenue Service views the assets in it as belonging to you. You pay taxes and so on just as if you held them in your name. If you hold the assets in an irrevocable trust, you have fully relinquished control over the assets and the trust arrangement. You can't even change beneficiaries. Because of this, irrevocable trusts are viewed as an entity separate from you, the grantor. It pays its own income taxes (unless the income doesn't remain in the trust but is distributed to beneficiaries). For estate tax purposes, however, the value of the assets is frozen at the date the assets are put in the trust. So, any appreciation will not increase the size of your estate. Thus, you might stay below the unified estate tax credit or at least maximize its effectiveness. One of the most effective strategies would be to put $2 million of assets in the irrevocable trust (the maximum amount of estate value sheltered by the unified estate tax credit). Afterward, you can then add $10,000 per year per beneficiary per donor (maximum tax-free gift), and as the assets grow your estate and its possible tax liability remain constant.

Testamentary Trust—Controlling Your Estate from the Grave

Testamentary trusts allow you to be more specific about who should get your assets—and when. Testamentary trusts don't exist until you die. They are established through instructions in your will. A prime example of such a trust is the QTIP Trust (Qualified Terminable Interest Property Trust), of particular interest to partners with heirs from prior marriages. A QTIP is ideally suited for satisfying, or at least controlling, the needs of your present partner and children from a previous marriage. Your current partner needs financial support, and your children need assurance that their step-parent isn't going to loot your estate or remarry and leave your estate to someone else. To satisfy your spouse's need for financial support after you die, this type of trust gives the surviving spouse or partner the income generated from the assets in the trust. To satisfy the children's concerns that their stepparent will spend your estate dry and leave nothing for them, the trust retains ownership of the assets and, as long as your current partner is not the trustee, your current partner has no control over the assets. Eventually, the assets pass to your children upon your current partner's death or to whomever else you designate.

In addition, the trust can have any number or type of clauses restricting access to the assets. For instance, you could specify that your spouse can live in the house but not own it. Or if she would like to move or sell it, the eventual beneficiaries, your children, would have to approve the sale. Keep in mind, in most states the spouse is entitled to some portion of the deceased spouse's estate even if the will does not specify so.

Charitable Remainder Trusts— For Giving and Receiving

Every now and then, and more frequently now that we've had huge run ups in stocks and now real estate, you'll read about huge donations made to a hospital, someone's alma mater, or even a poetry society. The donors are usually still alive and you wonder how rich they must be if they are able to give away so much money and still maintain their standard of living. More often than not, they do it through a Charitable Remainder Trust. A Charitable Remainder Trust allows you to donate assets to a nonprofit organization, receive the tax breaks from the donation, and still receive the income from the assets while you are alive. Amazing. And they make a lot of sense for those of us who aren't in the upper upper class, too. If you set the trust up as an irrevocable living trust, it gives you an immediate tax deduction for your charitable contribution and also allows you to receive the income from those assets while the assets are in the trust. In the trust agreement, you can arrange for the charity to get the trust's assets at some later date—after your death or even sometime later; maybe when your youngest child turns twenty-one. If you set it up as a testamentary trust (created upon your death), you can specify that the trust will provide income to your heirs for life and that the remainder of the trust's assets go to a nonprofit organization upon their deaths. This strategy, in addition to providing current income tax benefits and ongoing income, also reduces the value of your taxable estate. And it helps out a worthy cause.

An added bonus is the financial gain you receive. Charitable Remainder Trusts are ideal for older Americans who have assets that have greatly appreciated. They are getting to an age where they are more interested in current income from their investments rather than growth and appreciation. Ideally, they would like to sell the highly appreciated assets and replace them with bonds or dividend-paying stocks that will support their present cash needs. To sell the highly appreciated assets would incur a huge tax bill. By putting the assets in a Charitable Remainder Trust, instead, they eliminate the tax bill altogether. The Charitable Remainder Trust sells the assets, incurring no taxes because the beneficiary is a non-profit. The full value of the property remains in the trust, and the trust then is able to buy more income-generating assets and provide you with more income than if you had sold the assets rather than put them in the trust.

Hopefully, these issues and strategies now sound simple and straightforward to you. However, to accomplish that I have had to leave out the voluminous amount of details on the legal and tax issues that accompany estate planning. Issues constantly change, pitfalls loom if not done properly, and one size definitely does not fit all. I want you to understand the essence of these issues so that you have a sense of what might be available, but a treatise on all the types of trusts and all their permutations would fill an encyclopedia. I urge you to find a good estate-planning attorney who will listen and ensure that your wishes are carried out.

INVESTING TODAY—
WHAT YOU NEED
TO DO NOW

12

TIMES HAVE CHANGED

A lot of Americans grew up believing, or at least being told, that the way to get ahead in life was fairly simple. What you needed to do was to stay in school, do well in your classes, go on to a college, get a degree, and get a good job. A good job didn't necessarily mean an exciting job, or a job that you were passionate about, a good job was one that was safe, stable, and secure. I was fortunate that I didn't have parents who preached that particular chapter and verse of what could be thought of as the Old Ways. But I know a lot of people my age and a few years older who were taught that. The key was education—book learning leads to a job.

Unfortunately, not everyone was taught the importance of being financially savvy. I've touched on this idea before that our parents likely didn't sit us down and tell us how to budget, determine net worth, what the implications of various ownership instruments are, and so on. Some of us, whether by inclination or sheer inspiration or sometimes even perspiration, figured out the financial lessons life and our parents had to teach us. Others did not. At least not initially. And most people didn't really suffer because of that. They believed that the good job, putting money away in their savings accounts, maybe venturing into treasury notes or bonds, was going to provide for them a good retirement. Well, as Chapter 10 showed, we need to do a lot more to prepare for retirement than our parents did. Those pension plans are either cut back or nonexistent, a savings account doesn't even earn you a pittance anymore (it's more like a pit you can bury your money in), Social Security may or may not be there to help finance your so-called Golden Years, and even that job security you were counting on de-materialized in the age of mergers, downsizing (no, that's not quite right, how about "right-sizing") the global economy, and other factors.

Wages trying to keep pace with rising costs, the easy availability of credit, a generation often referred to as the "Me Generation"—which really meant, "Me Want, Me Deserve, Me Going to Buy," all contributed to a consumer culture that was out of control. This all meant that a generation of Americans was raised believing that their financial lives didn't hold the promise of a future better than what their parents had experienced. Not for a long time had a generation faced this painful reality. So what do we do when the "work hard, save wisely" advice of a previous generation has failed us?

To be honest, that advice didn't fail all of us—only some of us. For a long time, a relatively small group of people knew the key to maintaining and increasing wealth. Ironically, some call them the "Wealthy." How did many of them get that way? To some of us it will seem like a new idea, but the truth is, to borrow a commercially worn phrase, "They did it the old fashioned way." In other words, they invested it in the market. For some of you, this notion of investing is as commonplace as the idea that you have to keep breathing to survive. It's a normal part of your life. For others, this is a somewhat new and frightening concept, too much like gambling for you to be comfortable with.

A BRIEF CONCESSION TO THE PAST

It should come as no surprise either that given how much the world has changed in our lifetimes that my own attitude and beliefs about investing have changed as well. They should, right? To sit back and hope that what got you through one set of circumstances a few years ago is going to work in this set of circumstances is unwise. Remember, the definition of insanity is doing the same thing over and over again and expecting a different result. Well, the same is true of investing. You have to adapt, adopt, and become adept at doing those first two things quickly.

In my previous books, you will find some very important information about the basics of investing. I have defined terms, explained how you value different assets, and gone over the basics of how to invest. In this book, I want to get more into the strategy of investing and how I've reevaluated how to successfully invest.

I used to believe in buy and hold and asset allocation. You can look at the stock market's returns of 28.5 percent from 1995 to 1999, its return of 18.4 percent during all of the 1990s, or its average return since 1926 of 10.4 percent and say, "I'll take it." But, the Internet bubble and September 11th were wake-up calls for all of us. We don't preach, "Past returns are no guarantee of future performance" for no reason. At some point, many investors lost sight of this. Their most recent experience colored their vision of the future.

I began to advise my clients to move out of stocks and into cash shortly after the market began to leak air. Most of them complied. But the business manager of one client, a famous actress, insisted that she stick with some stocks that had done well in the past. "She's young and has plenty of time," he said, "The stocks will come back." This is the classic mantra of buy-and-hold, of course. It's a good mantra and one that I used to say myself. As much as I argued that times had changed, the business manager would not budge. The actress lost a bundle.

The old model of asset allocation—in other words diversifying your investments—that I preached along with most of my colleagues for many years, frankly doesn't seem to be working anymore either. It was fine to have a car in every lane when all the vehicles were gassed up and raring to go. But why stick with an investment that's stalled and being lapped? I had no problem advising my clients to put all of their money into cash investments returning 4 or 5 percent when the stock market was losing value across the board. Why put your eggs in so many baskets that your portfolio is doomed to mediocrity? That 10.4 percent per year was nice while it lasted, but it will not be the norm from here on out. I want to show you some of the issues that illustrate why I believe that the twin mantras of buy and hold and asset allocation should not be blindly heeded.

A PRELIMINARY NOTE ON RISK

Risk is a matter of control. Some of you are control freaks. You can admit that about yourself, and that's good, because admitting it gives you a feeling of control. Others of you are willing to let go a greater degree, and you find yourself on a sliding scale somewhere from reluctant but able to completely laissez-faire—a word with French origins, which should mean, "I don't care," but actually loosely translates to "hands off." No surprise that my clients all fit somewhere on that spectrum. Some people love the notion of investing being a kind of game. They love it because they believe they understand the rules and strategies so well that they have no other recourse but to win. They believe that they are in control, so consequently, they view investing as having less inherent risk than others who don't feel that they're in control—remember our Texas Slims and our Worst-Case Scenarists? I don't believe that you can judge one or the other in terms of courage. What really separates them is their willingness to give up control or to understand fully how their perceptions of control influence their behavior.

For example, I have a client I will call Roberta. Roberta's a Worst-Case Scenarist of the highest order—she can read into the phases of the moon a certain and swift downturn in the market, she reads the availability of parking spaces like they are tea leaves foretelling the imminent doom of her latest business ventures, and getting her to invest in anything besides a T-bill wasn't like pulling teeth, it was like convincing an A-list star to give up his dental implants. Alan is a classic Texas Slim. He loves the action, is constantly on the phone wanting me to update his portfolio, has one ear permanently to the ground listening for tips and insights, and if he ain't trading, he ain't happy. Guess which one rides a motorcycle, an activity many would say is "risky." That's right, I probably gave it away and you figured it was the opposite of what you would expect. So, how about this: Why does Roberta not see the risk inherent in two-wheeled locomotion?

And, as a bonus question, why in the heck does Alan HATE roller-coasters?

And, as a super bonus question, why won't I gamble and my husband loves to?

Come to think of it, why won't I go on a roller-coaster either?

The answer is partly the contradictory nature of human beings, but more important for our purposes is Roberta's perceptions about control. To her, operating a motorcycle isn't inherently dangerous because she trusts her own skill, feels that she has enough room and a motorcycle is agile enough to move quickly in a traffic lane to avoid other vehicles, and if she's going to go, she'd rather do it on her terms. Alan hates roller-coaster rides for the same essential reason—he's not in control. He loves the speed and whoops and inversions of investing (though it's never really all that thrilling) because he is in control of his financial destiny. He feels that he has the skills and knowledge, and he trusts that he was smart enough to find someone to help him who has additional skills and knowledge to augment his own, so that he can maneuver his money to avoid being splatted just as Roberta does. You would never catch him on a motorcycle though.

So, risk is all about perception, as is much of life, and the illusion/reality of control. That probably explains why one of my ninety-year-old clients insists that all her money be in the stock market. Look at it from this perspective: Is trusting that you are going to have enough money for retirement available through savings, pensions, and Social Security any less risky than investing in the market? Who among us really has any say so over the future of Social Security? So that's not the best example, but the point is that controlling your own financial future makes good sense. Whether that means what option to choose when it comes time to select who will manage your 401(k) contributions or choosing a financial advisor or selecting stocks to purchase, when you are the one making the decisions you are eliminating a good portion of the risk.

I don't intend for this to appear like it is all psychological sleight of hand. I'll go back to another mantra: Knowledge is Power. Power is Control. Control is Security. Security is Bliss.

CATCHING UP MEANS AT SOME POINT YOU'VE CAUGHT UP

Since 1982, the stock market has accumulated extraordinary gains as it played catch up. You used to be able to look at the obviously undervalued market and throw darts to pick winners. Led by new technologies, population trends, and a better understanding of valuing companies, just about everywhere you looked you found the proverbial low-hanging fruit—easy pickings. You bought, you held, and you allocated assets to multiple markets and instruments so that you didn't miss out on the next hot market. Changes since 2001 have shown us that it won't be so easy anymore.

I don't mean to throw out all the rules of the past. Some still make sense, and I'll let you know what they are. There are some circumstances that require a different approach, such as retirees depending on a steady, predictable income. I will show you how to combine technical analysis (when to buy and sell) with fundamental analysis (what to buy and sell).

The gospel of diversification was drummed into me when I was a young financial advisor, and I went out into the world and spread the word for many years. But asset allocation isn't what it used to be. The reason is simple: The marketplace isn't what it used to be. If you've allocated your assets at 60 percent stocks, 30 percent bonds and 10 percent cash and a year later discover that your stocks are doing so well that they now account for 70 percent of your assets, why in the name of solid profit would you want to slow your momentum by "rebalancing" your portfolio? If you're riding a loser, by all means tug on the reins and leap off. If you're riding a winner, though, why bail out unless there's some indication that your asset is fading in the stretch? We'll talk about how to do this, including which indicators bear watching.

Another note to keep in mind. In this age of instant access to reams of data that would have once taken an analyst, days, weeks, or even months to put together, we have it available at the click of a mouse button and on television. As a result, we have so many more people trading and investing than ever before. Factor in all the people with 401(k) plans who tweak their accounts as often as they glance at the clock wondering when their workday will end, and you have an enormous increase in trading volume. The market is just that much more volatile than it was before, and buy and hold and volatility just don't mix.

RISKS ON THE HORIZON—
CAMELOT NO MORE?

As I sit down to write this section, I see a mixed bag of economic news:

- Gold has just reached a twenty-five-year high. The huge run-up in the late 1970s and early 1980s as Paul Volcker and the Fed battled runaway inflation with double-digit interest rates (does anyone remember 18 percent interest rates?) was the last time gold was at these levels.

- Silver is soaring toward levels not seen since the Hunt brothers tried to corner the market in the 1970s.

- Oil is at $75 a barrel even though supplies and inventories are rising. Speculators and fear seem to be driving this market more than fundamentals.

- To stave off deflation and possible depression, former Federal Reserve chairman Alan Greenspan inflated the money supply so much that prices soared. Now the Fed has had to raise rates sixteen straight times since beginning to tighten the money supply in June 2004.

- All that liquidity/money supply had to go somewhere. Leery of the stock market, investors went crazy for real estate. Prices soared. Nearly one-third of all residential sales were investments. People bought with zero-down and other risky mortgages. Now, $4 trillion of those exotic mortgages are set to have their interest rates reset at much higher levels. Foreclosures are already up 72 percent so far in 2006.

- Popular areas, like Phoenix, have seen 25 percent per year appreciation over the past five years.

- Natural resource prices have boomed with record housing starts and strong industrial production.

- Record trade and budget deficits continue.

- The Dow is flirting with its all-time high reached during the Internet bubble. For eight years you've been holding your breath and hoping to get even again.

- General Motors and Ford are the subjects of bankruptcy rumors.

- Established, high-flying tech stock leaders are starting to show their age and vulnerability.

- The overall market no longer looks undervalued. It may even be overvalued. The no-brainer 1980s and 1990s catch-up bull markets aren't likely to repeat now.

- Hedge funds have gotten bigger and more powerful. At times, they seem to be the ones unnaturally moving various markets.

- Google represents the Internet bubble all over again. Its price assumes that its earnings will grow 20 percent every year for the next twenty-five years.

- Iran has nuclear capabilities. They are talking about sharing it with other poor countries. The United Nations is getting ready to sanction Iran, which may lead to further problems.

- Iraq is embroiled in Civil War. The Middle East continues to become more unstable.

- Bird flu, mad cow disease, and SARS have caused concern about a pandemic.

- Immigration/assimilation are big issues in the United States and France.

- Another African genocide is taking place, this time in the Sudan.

I don't mean to scare you with what is on this list. I am not saying that the market is a bad investment. I'm just saying that it requires different thinking and a more careful approach in order to succeed. A lot of question marks and a lot of possible shocks to the global system make dartboard investing dangerous.

WILL HISTORICAL RETURNS CONTINUE?

Nearly eighty years of stock market data seems like enough to draw some conclusions about the market. And if you're interested in the very long run, maybe it is. However, remember our ubiquitous legal disclaimer about the past not representing the future. The question is: Is the past a good representation of what we're facing today? I don't believe it is. I have three major reasons for my stance:

1. We have just benefited from a perfect storm of factors beneficial to the market.

2. Those factors will not be sustained.

3. Historically, such high valuations have been followed by weak performance.

Figures 12-1 and 12-2 show this trend. Figure 12-1 shows the Dow Jones Industrial Average from 1928 to 1999.

If you take just a cursory look at the chart, you may think that being in the market the entire time was a walk in the park. Year in and year out getting your 10.4 percent return. But if you take a closer look, you'll see that nearly all of that return happened between 1982 and 1999.

As you can see, if you'd been in the market during that entire period, you'd have years of near-stagnant returns and then achieved considerable gains if you got in any time after World War II. The

FIGURE 12-1. **Dow Jones Industrial Average from 1928 to 1999.**

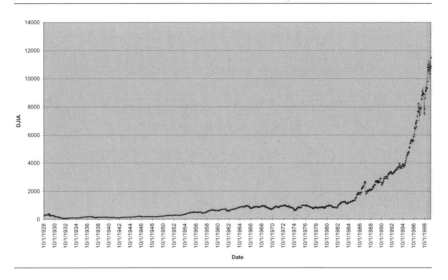

FIGURE 12-2. **Dow Jones Industrial Average from 1982 to 1999.**

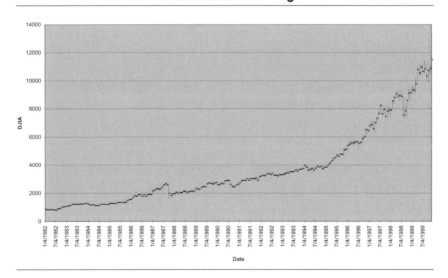

closer to 1982 you got in, the more meteoric the rise. Figure 12-2 illustrates what this boom period looked like.

The period from 1982 to 1999 was ideal for financial markets:

- Falling interest rates benefited expansion.

- We came down from high inflation rates of 1960s and 1970s to low rates throughout the period.

- Easy money coupled with "monetization" of homes (home equity lines) and cars (leasing) as well as charge card ubiquity unleashing more money into the economy. Rising two-income families also helped.

- The government was willing to let budget and trade deficits soar at stratospheric rates to support the economy.

- Improved and stable tax environment made capital investment less risky.

- Strong demographics as Baby Boomers went through the spending and savings phases of their lives.

- Technological breakthroughs fueled new industries and transformed the economy.

- Aggressive accounting policies raised earnings.

- More information about the market and better understanding of how to value assets.

- We were coming off a period of dismal market performance. Valuations began the period at low levels. The Dow was lower in 1982 than it was in 1973.

- The Standard & Poor's 500 index rose twelve-fold from that low in 1982 to its high in 1999. Price-to-earnings ratios tripled.

CAN THESE FACTORS BE SUSTAINED?

The question is not whether current levels can be sustained, (although that is also debatable), but whether the huge rate of improvement in these factors can be duplicated. Can taxes be reduced at the same rate? Can interest rates fall as precipitously as they did? Can inflation be cut by as much? I think all of that is unlikely. Can market valuations increase as much—triple from around twenty to sixty! The Gen-X cohort is as large in number as the Baby Boomers, but on a percentage basis it does not have the same financial impact that Baby Boomers had—they simply don't earn as much, spend as much, invest as much as Boomers. Can all of these beneficial factors duplicate their astounding performance of the past twenty-odd years? Think of it in terms of a growth stock. In the beginning, adding $1 billion of sales to a $500 million company is a marvelous 200 percent growth rate. As the company grows to $30 billion, that $1 billion sales increase adds up to only a 3.3 percent growth rate. The bigger the starting base, the less the impact for same effort.

We've caught up and even surpassed previous markets. Assets are fully valued, if not overvalued. We're now at a crossroads. Will things return to their previous levels or will we be able to sustain our peak levels? What will happen as Boomers move into the disinvesting stage of their lives? Can another part of the economy pick up the slack?

DOES BUY AND HOLD
HOLD UP ANYMORE?

If your grandparents were prescient enough in 1926 to invest in one of the few stocks that has survived and prospered through 2005; theoretically, excluding dividends, it would be worth 98 times what was paid for it back then. That's the thrust of the buy and hold argument. If you wait long enough, you'll get that long-run average year in and year out. That's OK for a college endowment fund or for a large foundation, but not all of us can afford to have an eighty-year time horizon. We have college to pay for and retirement to fund. Our time horizons are only ten or twenty years. Forty years maximum for a fortunate few.

Remember the people I mentioned earlier who were calculating how 10.4 percent can get them to retirement? There are even more people looking at negative returns over the past eight years who are asking themselves how much they now have to earn over their limited time horizon in order to compensate for the last eight years of seeing no return on their investment. Lest you forget, it wasn't all smooth sailing for your grandparents either.

Figure 12-3 illustrates that prior to the post-World War II expansion, investors were like ocean-going sailors caught in the doldrums—not much wind in your sails to move you either up or down the coast.

The Post War run-up was a real boon to investors, but that came

FIGURE 12-3. **Dow Jones Industrial Average from 1928 to 1965.**

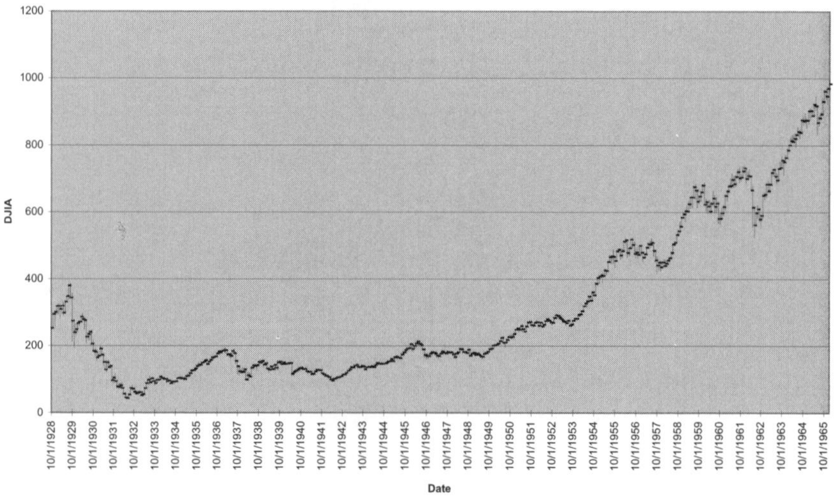

to a screeching halt around 1965 or 1966. Many attribute this to the Kennedy assassination, government spending on social programs and Vietnam, and other factors. It was as if the wave crested and tossed our ship onto a sand bar where we bobbed and weaved a bit on the tides, but made no real progress. And even with the post-war run-up, investors prior to the Depression were still underwater by a considerable amount. Figure 12-4 illustrates this stagnant period.

FIGURE 12-4.   Dow Jones Industrial Average from 1964 to 1981.

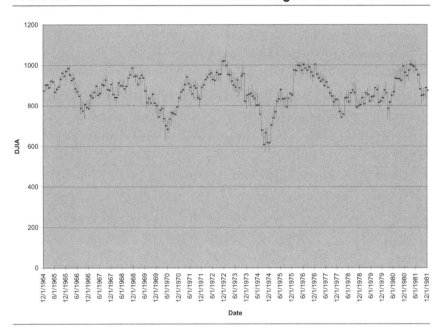

There were many nerve-wracking years:

- From 1929 to 1948 stocks plunged dramatically (86 percent from 1929 to 1937 and 54 percent again in 1938), recovered significantly by 1937, but by 1948 were still down more than 50 percent from the 1929 peak. Many people call 1966 the cyclical peak of the post-war boom market. The next decade saw the most severe bear markets in the last half of this century. From 1969 to 1970 it fell 34 percent. During 1973 and 1974 it lost 47 percent. Between December 1968 and December 1974, the unweighted value line index of 1,700 stocks lost more than 74 percent.

- The period from 1973 to 1982 was poor for the market. The Standard & Poor's 500 was lower in August 1982 than in January 1973. Adjusted for inflation, the results were far worse.

- Excluding dividends, it took twenty-four years to regain the value it had at the 1929 peak.

- Excluding dividends again, it took twenty-seven years to recover to its peak 1966 value.

If your grandparents needed to cash out at any time during one of those bleak periods they could very well have had less available than they had put in.

What if you had only twenty years to save for retirement? What were your chances of coming out ahead? To give you an idea, Figure 12-5 looks at all the possible twenty-year periods since 1919.

The chart in Figure 12-5 shows that you had a 50 percent

FIGURE 12-5. Twenty-year rolling returns of the Dow Jones Industrial Average, from 1919 to 2003, ranked by decile.

Decile	Range of Total Returns		Avg. Return For Decile	Avg. PE at Start
Lowest 10%	1.20%	4.50%	3.20%	19
2	4.50%	5.20%	4.90%	18
3	5.20%	5.40%	5.30%	13
4	5.40%	5.80%	5.50%	12
5	5.90%	7.20%	6.50%	15
6	7.20%	8.80%	8.10%	16
7	9.00%	9.30%	9.20%	16
8	9.40%	10.80%	10.20%	12
9	11.00%	11.90%	11.70%	12
Highest 10%	11.90%	15.00%	13.40%	10

Source: Crestmont Research

chance of making only 6.5 percent (pretax and pre-inflation). Your chances of making the long-run average of 10.4 percent were less than 1 in 4. In addition, the periods with the highest returns started with the lowest price-to-earnings ratios. We are now at price-to-earnings levels exceeding 20, even higher than the periods when returns were lowest. So, your chance of attaining historical average returns is cut even further. When you start out at high valuation levels it is difficult to get even average returns. Results for shorter periods are even worse.

To recap, the rosy picture history paints isn't as rosy as it seems when you break it down. We're still at a high point in valuations, so history indicates that our future outlook isn't as rosy as the historical averages would indicate. So discount those returns even more. Buy and hold works well if you are lucky enough to buy when stocks are out of favor or you can wait eighty years, but when you buy at rich valuations or need to cash out in the short or medium-term, you might want to try some other strategy.

AND ONE MORE THING . . .

I've picked on buy and hold enough. What about my gripe with asset allocation? Many of the same arguments apply to asset allocation. Over long periods it might make sense, but over shorter periods it can work to your disadvantage. Just as the stock market in general goes through cycles, each of its sectors goes through its own cycles.

Putting certain sectors or assets in your portfolio merely because you want to diversify is a ticket to mediocrity. The dogs will drag down your stars. If you've identified a fundamental trend, stick with it until the trend changes. During a period of falling interest rates—publicly traded real estate, homebuilders, and building material suppliers among others will do well. In times of rising rates—banks and discount stores might be the ticket. You have to adjust to the conditions.

Different asset classes, such as real estate and commodities, go through their own cycles, too. With falling interest rates, look to real estate and natural resources.

I don't think it makes sense to rebalance your portfolio just to make sure that you are in all asset classes. If you've got a winner, why sell prematurely just to adhere to some arbitrary percentage allocations? Of course, huge concentrations can be risky—ask anyone who invested solely in tech stocks or who put all their profit sharing in their company's own stock and then lost their job and their savings. But if you really want to continue to believe in asset allocation, at least don't start selling winners to move your percentages around 5 percent or 10 percent.

Remember the behavioral finance studies we talked about in part I of the book? One of those studies showed that those stocks we sell do better the next year than those we hold. The same theory applies to the market as a whole. Out-of-favor stocks consistently do better than the prior period's high fliers. Why sell stocks based on asset allocation rules or just on hunches? Unless you have a good methodology or a clear view of changes in the market, let your profits run.

Given all the large scale financial and political conditions I listed earlier and the fact that the market is fully valued, I believe we're at a real crossroads. I think the upside is tempered, stagnant overall growth in value is likely, and falling values are definitely possible. Spreading your money across the entire market just to keep your hand in the game won't accomplish what it did in the past. It more likely will lead to mediocrity as your winners are drowned out by the losers. Being more selective is the key.

And if all this sounds like it's a little too involved and you'd rather your money work and not you. In the next chapter, I provide a brief look at mutual funds—an investment tool that spreads the risk, reduces your work load, and allows you to benefit from the experience and savvy of professionals. In addition, I provide specific recommendations for the different financial temperaments, so that you and your partner can assess which strategy works comfortably for the both of you—a fine topic for your State of the Financial Union Meeting.

WHAT TO INVEST IN NOW

W hich stock should I buy? I'm sure when you buy a home you will put a lot of thought and investigation into finding just the right one for you and your family. Among other things, you investigate the area, check the reputation of the builder, determine the quality of the schools, ensure that the quality of life you want is available nearby, and listen for information about the local government and future developments. I doubt that you'd want to buy a house on a quiet street that is planned to become a four-lane main thoroughfare. When you invest in the stock market, you go through a similar process. I've practiced and preached fundamental analysis from the beginning, and I still believe in analyzing stocks on their fundamentals as a filter screen of all possibilities. I look at such things as:

- Do they operate in a good market with successful products?

- Are they well-managed?

- Do they have some protective competitive advantage?

- Do they have the financial wherewithal to operate successfully?

- Are they fundamentally sound rather than built on some sort of gimmick?

You can rely on others for this analysis—brokerage houses and banks, Internet sources, and independent research firms like Value Line and Morningstar provide such analysis. If you want to do it yourself, you can collect the information from 10-Ks, the Internet, news services, and other providers. No matter which direction you choose to go in search of information, just be certain that you do it. Once again: Knowledge is Power. Power is Control. Control is Security. Security is Bliss.

Fundamental analysis will give you a list of what to invest in. But, just as importantly, you have to decide *when* to invest in those promising companies you've uncovered. It would be nice if all you had to do was locate a stock with solid fundamentals, invest your retirement money in it, and live happily ever after with your 10.4 percent per year reward for good research. Unfortunately, it doesn't work that way. Other investors are also looking at the companies on your list and making their determination of its value. They may value it higher than you do. There may be many more potential buyers than there are sellers—just as can happen with consumer products like the hottest new televisions or game consoles. It does no good to invest in a fundamentally sound company at the top of a cycle when it is fully valued or in high demand. Even the best stocks go through periods of over- and underestimation of their prospects. Industries and sectors go through cycles of popularity and neglect. Some of it is based on the business cycle and fundamentals and some of it is sheer emotion. Also, great stocks often get lumped together with the industry or sector they operate in, even if they don't share their brethren's outlook.

Rather than lament the inefficiency, randomness, and craziness of the market, use it to improve your returns. Many methods exist to time your investment purchases and sales more efficiently. I happen to use point and figure technical analysis because it boils the supply and demand and emotional aspects of the market down to an understandable and time-tested charting system. I can use it to find entry points as well as to know when to sell. But other methods exist, and you should find one that fits your temperament, available time, and abilities. Many great online and written resources are out there to explain each of the methods, and I recommend that you investigate and test several before you actually use them.

I think that any investor should read *The Wall Street Journal*, *Money* magazine, *Smart Money*, and *Kiplinger's Personal Finance*. Each in its own way has excellent insight into, and great information on, the world of investing. Among the plethora of online resources, it's hard to beat Yahoo! Finance, Morningstar, Inc., TheStreet.com, and Bankrate.com. Although the last of these is not specifically investment related, it gives you great information about credit card interest rates, mortgage rates, and so on—it's a great personal finance tool.

I know that charting and the like smack of black magic to some. I agree that fundamentals *should* rule the market. Remember, however, our discussions of behavioral finance. Studies and simple quizzes demonstrated that emotions and irrationality play a large part in our financial decisions. Charting and other so-called technical analysis methods attempt to capture those market emotions and mispricings and turn them to your advantage.

MUTUAL FUNDS AS YOUR INVESTMENT VEHICLE

Very few people have the time, knowledge, and energy to do all the analysis and investment decision making on their own. And, frankly, it gets harder and harder to outfox the market. Unless you're willing to view it as your second job or serious hobby, I suggest mutual funds as the best method for investing in nearly every

category of investment assets. They provide professional investment management and are easy to find and invest in. They are
available in just about any flavor to suit your needs and risk profile
and are cost-efficient.

Each mutual fund is professionally managed, so you don't need
to worry about picking the right securities and constantly monitor-
ing them. No need to read 10-Qs, earnings estimates, and other
news affecting the companies you own. The fund managers and
their staffs pore over earnings reports, talk to securities analysts
and company executives, and keep up with the many political, social, and economic events affecting the markets, and they make
decisions about what to buy and when.

With mutual funds, you automatically get a diversified portfolio
of stocks or bonds for a relatively small investment. I've been
preaching against diversification, but only in the sense of spreading
your money around in many different arenas. The diversification
that mutual funds can provide is actually good. It reduces your risk
exposure to a single stock or bond. Choose a fund that specializes
in a particular asset, company size, industry, sector, country, and so
on, and let the fund managers pick the best stocks or bonds from
that group. You are not diversifying away the returns you expect
from that category you have chosen, you are only limiting your exposure to one particular company in that category—which is a good
idea.

You can invest odd-dollar amounts and on any schedule you
like. If you are contributing part of every paycheck, you'll end up
with lots of odd dollar amounts coming into your account every
couple of weeks or so. If you were investing in stocks or bonds directly, you'd need to wait until you had a sufficient amount—usually
multiples of $1,000 for bonds and one hundred–share lots for
stocks—before you could invest. With mutual funds, you can invest
odd dollar amounts and they get invested as soon as they get into
the account. This can happen because the fund managers pool all
the investments that come in to purchase stocks or bonds, they

don't buy them specifically with your money or just for your account.

Lastly, and very important for our purposes, you can move your money around as market conditions change. I'm not advocating day trading, and I don't think any mutual funds would allow it, anyway. But as the situation changes you can easily move your money from one fund to another. These days, most funds are offered by a large management firm that offers a large array of funds, a so-called family of funds. For instance, most offer the basic types of funds as well as industry-specific, objective-specific, and life-stage funds. If you decide that you want to switch from a financial services investment fund to a real estate fund, you should be able to stay within the same family. Moving from one fund to another within the family is easy and nearly always free. If you move to another family of funds, some firms assess fees to redeem your investment in their funds within a certain period of time—as short as thirty days for some and five years for others. Make sure you understand and read the prospectus and know the whole spectrum of funds offered before you commit to a family.

Which Mutual Funds?

Amazingly, there are now more mutual funds than actual stocks on the major exchanges. It can get pretty complicated deciding which funds to buy unless you're organized about it and have specific criteria. Services such as Morningstar exist to rate the return and risk performance of funds. I'd like to add a few of my own criteria that make sense in this volatile environment:

1. Of course, a good performance record without taking undue risk is a given. Look for managers who have done well through a full business cycle. Even three years of good performance is not sufficient proof of good investment management.

2. Find a family of funds with no or limited redemption penalties. You won't be moving your money around daily or even monthly, but you will need to be ready to change funds as the market changes.

3. It's okay to pay more for EXTRA return, but make sure you get your money's worth. Factor all fund expenses into your return calculations when you choose which fund to use. If we were investing in generic index funds I would certainly tell you to go with the lowest expense fund. You may end up using some specialty funds as you ride market trends, and some of those categories may have a wide range of return and expense profiles. Don't choose merely by expense ratios. Decide based upon the after-expense return.

4. To reduce expenses, look for a family of funds that allows free movement of funds within the entire family and has a broad array of funds that will fit your need to move around as the economy shifts.

5. Which sectors you should target depends on your reading of the market's next direction. At times, bonds or real estate funds make sense. At other times, a technology fund might be in order. In general,

   a. Avoid broad market index funds. They are too diversified to meet our needs.

   b. Value funds, which look for good companies that happen to be out of favor at the time, profit from cyclicality and the behavioral finance tenets we examined earlier.

   c. Lastly, don't chase returns. Don't choose the sector or fund that did the best last year. It's probably too late to get on that bandwagon. Anticipate the next move rather than getting on the backend of the existing wave. That's usually the riskiest time to invest.

By knowing where you fit on the risk scale, you and your partner can better understand why there's not just volatility in the stock market, but also in your relationship. As we've seen throughout this book, money matters are always entwined with emotional matters. What you think you know is often expressed in how you feel. As logical as you may try to be, it's not always possible to separate your anxieties and your past from your present. As always though, if you have the knowledge about your respective levels of risk tolerance, you then have the power to take control over your decisions, make those decisions securely, and enjoy the bliss that comes from knowing the two of you have worked together toward a shared future with your best feet forward.

ARCHETYPAL INVESTMENT RECOMMENDATIONS

The money personalities that you discovered through the quiz in chapter 2 can have distinct approaches to investing. Ritz-Carltons might be performance chasers—seeking out the hottest stock, sector, or manager so that they can impress their friends with their savvy—even if the cost of their investment decisions is high. After all, the finer things in life cost money, whether it's a bottle of wine or shares of Google. Worst-Case Scenarists might not even invest at all—they could choose to put all their money in the bank or in a safe spot in the house. That's extreme, but they're likely to play it safe in bonds or perhaps even a mutual fund and choose the most conservative holdings. Texas Slims swing for the fences—taking on too much risk in order to get that one big payoff that will keep them in the money for life. None of these approaches is optimal, and each should be modified to get you closer to a more efficient approach to investing.

It would be nice to be able to list a perfect portfolio for each personality and then let you just follow that. Unfortunately, too many other factors go into crafting a proper portfolio for me to give you a one-size-fits-all model. Instead, let's talk a little about one of the primary issues I use in constructing a portfolio for a client. Then we can discuss some of the ways these personalities can move toward an ideal portfolio.

One of the critical factors a knowledgeable investment advisor will use to construct a suitable portfolio for you is your age. The widely held and followed theory of life stage investing states that it is best to start your investing life a little aggressively and as you age and reach various stages in your life you should reduce your risk somewhat, and when you reach retirement your portfolio should favor less risky investments such as bonds and utilities. One old-fashioned version of the appropriate percentages of stocks and bonds by your age is shown in Figure 13-1.

There is more to the theory than just age. Diversification of your investment portfolio is a good thing no matter how old you are. The old maxim of not putting your eggs all in one basket pays off in the investing world. You're taking too much risk if you have all your money riding on one stock. Sure, there are some people

FIGURE 13-1. Life cycle investment diversification.

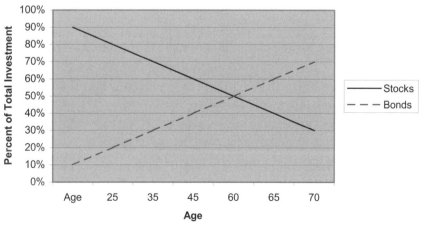

who have retired on their investments in Microsoft or General Electric, but more often than not by the time a company goes public all the people who are going to make ridiculous fortunes on the stock are already invested. They are founders, employees, venture capitalists, and other early-stage investors. And those stories don't happen as often as you might think. A venture capitalist is happy if one out of twenty investments makes it big. They rely on those one or two home runs in a career to keep them going through all the weak singles and strikeouts. They also spread their risk by joining with other investors to share their finds. You should take the same approach. Diversification is the act of spreading your money around. It means not having your stock portfolio concentrated in oil stocks or car manufacturers. Add some stocks that aren't tied to those industries or are influenced by other factors than those that influence the health of those industries.

The size of your portfolio and your income also bear upon how much risk you should take. The more money you have invested relative to your needs, both current funds and those set aside for retirement, the more risk you can take on without a loss to your entire aggressive portfolio being catastrophic. You have a large enough portfolio to at least live acceptably on the remaining holdings. Similarly, if you have a high enough income, over time you might be able to save enough to replace some of the losses, at least to a level that allows you to live acceptably.

Age factors into the diversification equation because of two of our old friends: the magic of compounding interest and the law of averages. Most of us will eventually stop working and need to live off our savings. The earlier we begin saving, the more we will end up with. The longer you allow your savings to grow, the more the math of compounding helps you. The meager 5 percent return you earn on your investment thirty years from now is actually a 20.6 percent return on your original investment, and your investment has grown 4.3 times. We've discussed this before, but the charts in Figures 13-2 and 13-3 show you again: the proof is in the com-

FIGURE 13-2. **The magic of compounding interest at 5 percent.**

	Beginning Amount	Earnings at 5%	Ending Total	Return on Your Original Dollar
1	$1.00	$0.05	$1.05	5.0%
2	$1.05	$0.05	$1.10	5.3%
3	$1.10	$0.06	$1.16	5.5%
4	$1.16	$0.06	$1.22	5.8%
5	$1.22	$0.06	$1.28	6.1%
6	$1.28	$0.06	$1.34	6.4%
7	$1.34	$0.07	$1.41	6.7%
8	$1.41	$0.07	$1.48	7.0%
9	$1.48	$0.07	$1.55	7.4%
10	$1.55	$0.08	$1.63	7.8%
11	$1.63	$0.08	$1.71	8.1%
12	$1.71	$0.09	$1.80	8.6%
13	$1.80	$0.09	$1.89	9.0%
14	$1.89	$0.09	$1.98	9.4%
15	$1.98	$0.10	$2.08	9.9%
16	$2.08	$0.10	$2.18	10.4%
17	$2.18	$0.11	$2.29	10.9%
18	$2.29	$0.11	$2.41	11.5%
19	$2.41	$0.12	$2.53	12.0%
20	$2.53	$0.13	$2.65	12.6%
21	$2.65	$0.13	$2.79	13.3%
22	$2.79	$0.14	$2.93	13.9%
23	$2.93	$0.15	$3.07	14.6%
24	$3.07	$0.15	$3.23	15.4%
25	$3.23	$0.16	$3.39	16.1%
26	$3.39	$0.17	$3.56	16.9%
27	$3.56	$0.18	$3.73	17.8%
28	$3.73	$0.19	$3.92	18.7%
29	$3.92	$0.20	$4.12	19.6%
30	$4.12	$0.21	$4.32	20.6%

pounding, and little increases in initial investments mean a lot down the road.

So, if you take a few chances early in your investing life, you still have the opportunity to benefit from the power of compounding interest over time.

Time also helps smooth out the rough spots. Over the long run, certain asset classes have had returns that differ based on their risk profiles. The longer you are able to hold an asset, the better your chances of getting that long-run average return. Over short peri-

FIGURE 13-3. The magic of compounding interest at 8 percent.

	Beginning Amount	Earnings at 8%	Ending Total	Return on Your Original Dollar
1	$1.00	$0.08	$1.08	8.0%
2	$1.08	$0.09	$1.17	8.6%
3	$1.17	$0.09	$1.26	9.3%
4	$1.26	$0.10	$1.36	10.1%
5	$1.36	$0.11	$1.47	10.9%
6	$1.47	$0.12	$1.59	11.8%
7	$1.59	$0.13	$1.71	12.7%
8	$1.71	$0.14	$1.85	13.7%
9	$1.85	$0.15	$2.00	14.8%
10	$2.00	$0.16	$2.16	16.0%
11	$2.16	$0.17	$2.33	17.3%
12	$2.33	$0.19	$2.52	18.7%
13	$2.52	$0.20	$2.72	20.1%
14	$2.72	$0.22	$2.94	21.8%
15	$2.94	$0.23	$3.17	23.5%
16	$3.17	$0.25	$3.43	25.4%
17	$3.43	$0.27	$3.70	27.4%
18	$3.70	$0.30	$4.00	29.6%
19	$4.00	$0.32	$4.32	32.0%
20	$4.32	$0.35	$4.66	34.5%
21	$4.66	$0.37	$5.03	37.3%
22	$5.03	$0.40	$5.44	40.3%
23	$5.44	$0.43	$5.87	43.5%
24	$5.87	$0.47	$6.34	47.0%
25	$6.34	$0.51	$6.85	50.7%
26	$6.85	$0.55	$7.40	54.8%
27	$7.40	$0.59	$7.99	59.2%
28	$7.99	$0.64	$8.63	63.9%
29	$8.63	$0.69	$9.32	69.0%
30	$9.32	$0.75	$10.06	74.5%

ods, you might earn far less or far more than that average, but over time things should even out. You could think of it in terms of selling your home. If you need to sell in a hurry, you will likely have to compromise on price and seriously consider offers that might be less than you think your home is worth just to get it sold quickly. However, if you are a patient seller, you can afford to wait until you get your price, the market improves, or the person who loves your home as much as you do shows up at your door. I always tell my clients, "It's not what you buy. It's when you sell that's important."

Diversification can also mean not just owning stocks. Put some money into bonds and real estate to add some stability and reduce risk. In fact, studies have been done that show that a diversified portfolio of stocks and bonds can outperform a portfolio of 100 percent stocks, plus reduce overall risk. Huge pension and endowment funds buy into very risky investments like real estate, venture capital, hedge funds, futures, options, and the like because studies also show that small investments in such very risky asset classes actually reduce the overall risk in their total portfolios, which are heavily loaded with stocks and bonds.

What does all this mean for your portfolio? Whether you are an Econo Lodger or a Drama Queen, you should ideally try to follow the general stock/bond diversification guidance in Figure 13-1. I realize that following such advice to the letter will be difficult for some of you, so take intermediate steps toward those guidelines. Here are some suggestions for how to do that based on your money personality.

Ritz-Carltons

You are probably enamored of the next new thing. You likely put your money in whatever the hot stock is, invest in the hot trend or gizmo, or follow the hot investment guru. Tips from club buddies or associates at work guide your investment decisions. Your chasing performance is not the best way to build a great portfolio. By the time the buzz has reached the masses, the time to buy has passed. And there are many more next big things that fizzle than there are next real things. Forget bragging at the club about your big winnings in one stock (while likely avoiding discussion of your many losers) and add some substance to your portfolio. Add some high-quality bonds. Look for strong and stable established stocks that can form the base of your portfolio, and depending upon your age, put 5 to 10 percent of your portfolio in some wild stocks to brag about.

Econo Lodgers

You are likely looking for safe, secure, and cheap. Index funds, which track the various stock market indexes, are right up your alley. Index funds will give you the average return of the market at very low cost. You won't be paying for some high-priced analysis and salesperson. On the other hand, you won't be getting the possibility of beating the market, either. That's not the point for you, anyway. You are the tortoise in the race, and with a little ramping up of your risk tolerance, the market should help you toward your goal. If you already are in a broad market index fund, don't get rid of that investment entirely but try to add a little risk by adding some investments in some of the segment index funds—whether small-cap stock indexes or certain industry sector indexes. Dip your toes and put some money in several in order to diversify.

Texas Slims

Everything that applies to Ritz-Carltons also applies to you—in spades (bad pun intended). Tone down the risk. For you, the motivation may be different, but the end result is the same. You don't need to hit a home run in order to win. Several singles are easier to get and will get you to the same place. The objective is to win, and statistics show that the best way to do so is by hitting singles. Put some bonds and Dow 30 stocks in your portfolio to form a base. Total withdrawal is probably not possible right away, so take a small portion (5 to 10 percent) of your portfolio and indulge your need for a bit of risk. Try to tone it down, though. They say that you hit a home run not when you try but when you have a fundamentally sound swing. Do your research before taking a flier. Really think about the fundamentals of investing. Play the odds when they are in your favor. Index funds in some of the minor indexes or a mutual fund that specializes in a special sector may allow you some gambling while still benefiting from investment management.

Worst-Case Scenarists

A true worst-case scenarist may not be investing at all. Hopefully, you've moved past that stage and now realize that you need to move beyond bank accounts and government bonds if you are to meet your retirement needs. The earlier you make the move to stocks the better off you will be. If you come to the sudden realization that at age fifty-five you aren't on track to have enough to retire you might be tempted to take on more risk than you can live with and is prudent—risking what you have amassed. Don't take too much but do it now. Dedicate 15 to 20 percent of your portfolio to investing in high-quality stocks—scions of the investment world. Use a method called dollar-cost averaging to slowly create the portfolio. This means that you employ the technique of buying a fixed dollar amount of a particular investment on a regular schedule, regardless of the share price. You buy more shares when prices are low, and fewer shares when prices are high. This is also referred to as the *constant dollar plan*. When you employ this plan, you don't take into account market conditions or your personal financial status. You make the purchases at regular intervals regardless. For you Worst-Case Scenarists, this takes the worry of guess work and market timing out of your mind.

Here's how it works: Take a small amount of the money you've set aside for the investment and periodically purchase shares until you've used up all the money. For instance, if you decide to put $50,000 into General Electric, but you're not sure about the short-term direction of the stock price, put $5,000 in right away, and every month or quarter buy another $5,000 worth of General Electric stock. Do this until you've invested the entire $50,000 you originally designated as a good amount to invest in General Electric. Subsequent investments should be made whether the price goes up or down. The only thing that should stop you from continuing to invest in General Electric is a fundamental change in the outlook for the company—if your original reason for thinking it a strong buy disappears. Dollar-cost averaging is a good way to reduce your risk of buying too high all at once. By investing a little over a length of time you average the price you pay. If prices fall, you won't be caught at the top, and if they rise you won't make as much but you'll have some protection.

In this way, you'll reduce your risk so that you can get comfortable with the idea of having an unknown return but knowing that time is on your side. Put another portion of your money into high-grade corporate bonds, also using dollar-cost averaging. They'll pay more than government bonds and still carry low risk of default.

Data Darlings

Analysis paralysis and control are your likely issues. I usually subscribe to the belief that the more information you have, the better a decision you can make. There is a law of diminishing returns, however. And if the search for more information stifles your ability to act, then it truly hampers your quest to build a retirement nest egg. As with Worst-Case Scenarists, if you haven't taken the plunge into stocks yet, this is your first order of business—but do so moderately. If you have moved past that step, try to overcome your anxiety by putting more of your money into mutual funds or hire an investment manager. Let them do the data analysis and pull the trigger on making investments. Find a manager who has been successful over the long run. Track how they do it and use their approach on the portion of your portfolio that you invest yourself. If it's a set of screens they use, vow to follow it without fretting over other issues. If it is a set of analysis tools, use that and stick to that formula. Just about any system is better than haphazard investing, and a system would seem to appeal to a data darling.

Drama Queens and Drama Kings

I hate to say it, but you Drama Queens and Drama Kings really need to be protected from yourselves. The hair-trigger response to events can result in getting into bad investments as well as getting out of good investments before you should. You might be taking on too much risk. You might be taking on too little risk. Risk is not the issue here. The real issue is what data you use to make decisions. It shouldn't be gut reactions but reasoned analysis of events. Otherwise, you risk being twisted in the wind, not getting anywhere, and making your broker rich on commissions from the churning of your portfolio you will end up doing. For you, professional management of the majority of your portfolio is essential. Pick a mutual fund or investment manager with whom you can develop rapport and trust and stick with it. Resist the temptation to bail out at the first bump in the road or when you have a sense of a better investment possibility elsewhere. If you really function best on that drama roller coaster, take a small portion of your portfolio, 5 to 10 percent, and use it as mad money.

Your task now is to find your bliss. I'm certain that you can see that you and your partner have a lot more to discuss—especially in light of the temperament-specific recommendations I've made above. As you begin your discussions, please keep in mind all the principles of good communication and honest negotiating that I laid out when talking about your Financial First Date and your Financial State of the Union Meetings. Now that you have a lot more information at your fingertips, these conversations are less likely to be chats and more likely to be work sessions in which you make important and informed decisions. At some point, you may even have to play the role of teacher if your partner isn't quite as familiar with all these concepts as you are now. Remember the old adage about giving a man a fish and teaching a man to fish.

Hmm. That reminds me. I wonder if Seattle's Pike Place Market is publicly traded? Better to sling salmon than bull, I suppose. I've got some homework to do—and so do you.

Epilogue
Parting Words

'm certain that by now you realize that sharing a financial life together is a little more complicated than simply saying, "I do," or otherwise verbally cementing your commitment to another person. I'm also certain that this came as no real revelation to you. That's as it should be. If there's one refrain that I want running through your head as you finish this book it's this: The more you prepare for life events, the better your outcome will be. I hope that the information contained in these pages will not only help you prepare for those bumps along life's road, but also show you how to achieve financial bliss!

We started this exploration by letting you know how important it is to understand yourself. You should now realize that as much as you may want to believe that you are a logical, rational, fact-crunching, results-spitting individual, the truth is that like most people, you can easily be an illogical, emotional, and miscalculating individual as well. That doesn't make you a bad person; it makes you a person. Just as important, we want you to understand the necessity of revealing to your partner, and having your partner reveal to you, aspects of your financial past that have a direct impact on how you handle, and how you feel about money today. Of course, as you well know, sharing of information and feelings is impossible unless you are able to communicate effectively, honestly, and thoroughly.

We also hope that you had some fun along the way—that in having your First Financial Date with your partner, you were able to deepen the trust between you, increase your level of financial intimacy, and in so doing, make your relationship and your bottom line richer and more rewarding.

NEXT STEPS

If you haven't undertaken some of the steps that we suggested (the Financial First Date, for instance), then that's the best place to start. Obviously, if you've read the material on retirement and investing, you know that time can be both your best friend (by letting the magic of compounding interest have a longer career to work) or it can be the ticking clock setting your heart racing. The sooner you and your partner settle in and begin having serious discussions about your financial goals and devising strategies to meet the time lines you've set for yourself, the sooner the two of you will be able to see positive results. Nothing like a little bit of positive reinforcement to keep the two of you motivated.

For those of you who find yourself particularly motivated or concerned about a particular aspect of financial planning mentioned here, doing additional research into some of the finer points of the various issues we explored—investing, taxes, insurance, mortgages, and so on—should prove rewarding. Whether that research constitutes doing reading in the library, surfing the Internet, talking with friends and family, or seeking out the advice of experts doesn't really matter. The key thing is that you will be breaking the circle of silence that surrounds financial matters. This circle of silence afflicts many families. Once that silence is broken, you'll be surprised (or maybe not since I'm telling you this here) how much information flows to you and through you.

I would be remiss if I didn't remind you one more time of the mantra that underpins this book: Knowledge is Power. Power is Control. Control is Security. Security is Bliss. I'm certain that you will experience moments of bliss throughout this process, as well as a few moments of frustration. That's to be expected when you're involved in any human endeavor. I wish you many rewards as you and your partner set out on this next phase in your life together.

ACKNOWLEDGMENTS

B ooks don't just happen. They are a result of collaboration, time, and sweat. The guy who did most of the sweating for *Financial Bliss* was my cowriter Gary Brozek. Thanks, Gary—I could not have done this without you.

I also want to give a special thanks to Brad Salter, Ph.D., who helped me conceive the idea for this book. Brad sees lots of couples in his Beverly Hills office, and it is no wonder that he saw the need for it!

My dear friend and mentor, Jonathan Barnett, must also get credit for the amazing work he shared with me on behavioral psychology with regard to money and spending.

I am very fortunate to have a team of professionals on whom I rely for legal and accounting opinions—Dennis Duitch, CPA, president of Duitch Consulting Group; Alin Wall, CPA, partner at RBZ Business Management, LLC; Tom Fehn, J.D., with Fields, Fehn, & Sherwin; and Steve Goldberg, J.D., with Russ, August, and Kabat.

I would like to give a special thanks to Stan Brooks, founder of my broker-dealer, Brookstreet Securities. Speaking of Brookstreet, thanks to all of you who tirelessly support my practice. Special thanks to Kathy McPherson, Rhoda Lawrence, Steve Skytte, Victor Chu, Tim Swanson, Russ Riccobono, Scott Magallanes, and Katie Cook.

My "home team" at Bambi Holzer Financial Group deserves medals for all of the hard work and long hours put in to make our business so successful. Parker Fehn, Chelsea Frazier, Chris Gordon,

Evan Marshall, Noel Boon, and Jeff Runyan—you're definitely GOLD to me!!

Elaine Floyd makes me sound better than I naturally do, with her magical mastery of the English language. She writes the way I think, and after twenty-plus years on my team, she's become a dear friend as well.

I'd like to thank my agents Jane Dystel and Miriam Goderich and my publishers at AMACOM; my editor Jacqueline Flynn; and Kama Timbrell, to whom I'll always be grateful for booking me on the *Today Show* for the first time when *Retire Rich* was published.

Most of all, I'd like to thank my wonderful friends and family. I can't imagine my life without all of you. Thank God I don't have to.

INDEX